THE ANCIENT FATHERS OF THE DESERT

THE ANCIENT FATHERS
OF
THE DESERT

**Translated Narratives from the *Evergetinos*
on Passions and Perfection in Christ**

by Archimandrite Chrysostomos

HELLENIC COLLEGE PRESS
Brookline, Massachusetts
1980

Published by the HELLENIC COLLEGE PRESS
50 Goddard Avenue
Brookline, Massachusetts 02146

Library of Congress Cataloging in Publication Data
Main entry under title:

The Ancient Fathers of the desert.

    Translation of Mikros Euergetênos.
    Includes index.
    1. Spiritual life--Orthodox Eastern authors.
I. Chrysostomos, Archimandrite.
BX382.M5413   248.4'819   80-28253
ISBN 0-916586-77-4
ISBN 0-916586-78-2 (pbk.)

Manufactured in the United States of America

For my spiritual Father, who is far
above me, and for those under me,
who far surpass me

TABLE OF CONTENTS

INTRODUCTION

As Eastern Orthodoxy grows among English-speaking peoples, Western Christians are becoming increasingly familiar with Christianity's oldest tradition, with the Church which claims to bring to modernity the very spirit and essence of the Apostolic Church. Yet this familiarity, as flattering as it might be to a venerable faith which has seen the ancient witness of millions upon millions of its children fade into social and historical obscurity in the West, is fraught with danger. For, paradoxically, the growth of Eastern Orthodoxy is occurring at a time when Orthodox spirituality is at a particular low. A vast majority of the Church struggles in Eastern Europe under the yoke of political persecution. In many places the simple discussion of Orthodoxy is perilous. Monasticism, often characterized by Eastern Fathers as the barometer by which Orthodox spiritual health is measured, is engaged in what appears to be a losing battle with contemporary social ideals and morality. Some of the most popular Orthodox theologians are tainted in their teachings by Western thought and by a non-Orthodox mentality. And with overwhelming sadness, we have seen, in the last several decades, the passing of many of the spiritual giants (Elder Philotheos Zervakos of Greece and Archimandrite Justin Popovich of Serbia, among others) who have been our living links to Orthodoxy's healthier spiritual past.

More importantly, Eastern Orthodox in the Western diaspora are struggling to establish a firm spirituality in the very midst of this world-wide crisis in the Church. The dangers of being cut

off from the more mature and developed centers of historical
Orthodoxy are heightened by the fact that in the West we have
the mere rudiments of traditional Orthodoxy. The Orthodox
goal *par excellence* is the deification of man, his union through
grace with Christ, and his attainment in this present life of the
virtues of Christian perfection -- sainthood. But the Saints,
these exemplars of Orthodoxy and the fulfilled Christian life,
fading as they are in world Orthodoxy, are hardly to be found
here in the West, however painful or discomforting this fact
may be. If we have attained any spiritual maturity, it is by merciful grace and at the cost of factionalism and spiritual pride
nurtured in an atmosphere which hardly augurs well of future
growth. The dangers which these weaknesses brew, as though
they were not dreadful enough for Orthodox Christians, are
compounded many times over when a non-Orthodox Westerner
wishes to learn or avail himself of the spirituality of the Orthodox East. Blinded by the fearful forces which bombard Orthodoxy in these days, an Orthodox Christian in the West is
hard-pressed to see his own way, let alone guide a stranger to his
path.

Yet, as always, though the darkness seems encompassing,
there is a glimmer of light to which we can turn. If the living
Fathers of the Church are disappearing and their availability to
some Orthodox is ever so slight, they have none the less left us,
as one spiritual man has assured me, "elders bound in leather
and gold." They have left to us their words and their written instructions. We can add, therefore, to the bare essentials of Orthodoxy present in the West, the thunderingly silent printed
patristic witness. We can begin slowly to see the essence and
substance of the unique truth that Orthodoxy is, not in
catechisms or statements of belief, but in actual practice. For,
ultimately Orthodoxy is not expressed only in correct beliefs,
doctrines, or dogmas. It is lived and felt and experienced.
Beliefs, doctrines, and dogmas reflect a "theology of facts," as
one great Church Father expressed it, and the *locus* of these
facts is personal spiritual experience and practice. Until we
know what we believe as it is expressed in lives lived and
transformed by real individuals, rather than from logical *dicta*

rising out of rigorous philosophical systems, we cannot adequately express to the Westerner the truth of the Orthodox Faith. And to know these real individuals, these incarnate pillars of philosophical truth, we must turn to the largely unknown spiritual treasures of Orthodoxy, the ascetic parables and writings of those who struggled with the passions for perfection in Christ.

There are two outstanding and indispensable compilations of the writings of the Holy Fathers of the Church which are most important for Orthodox in the West: the *Philokalia* and the *Evergetinos.* The *Philokalia,* a collection of writings by Fathers living approximately between 300 and 1400 A.D., contains exalted theological writings by some thirty Fathers. These writings are essentially instructions to monks and spiritual aspirants in methods by which, to quote the full title of the collection, "the mind is purified, illumined, and made perfect through practical and contemplative moral philosophy." It contains very advanced teachings ranging from advice on the proper control of the breath during prayerful contemplation to detailed instructions for the attainment of freedom from the passions. Though it has appeared in part in English, it is relatively unknown in its entirety to many Orthodox. Even in its Greek, Slavonic, and Russian editions, it is not widely read in modern times. The transition from an Orthodoxy lacking spiritual maturity and beset by formidable external foes to the perfection of the theoretical philosophy of the *Philokalia* is not an easy one and, even in translation, this collection is not a first solution to the spiritual naïveté of contemporary Orthodox.

The *Evergetinos* is probably the beginning point for Orthodox in the West who wish to capture something of the essence of their faith. If the *Philokalia* teaches pure prayer and the path to deification and union with God, the *Evergetinos* provides us with anecdotal evidence that the practice of Christian virtues, such as humility, chastity, love for our neighbor, and submission to the will of God, can bring us to the brink of the ultimate encounter with the divine by which we are elevated to the philosophical and higher struggle for perfection. If from the *Philokalia* we are instructed in the philosophical way to perfection, in the *Evergetinos* we are guided to the pragmatic life of humility and self-control (composure), the indispensable requisites for the more advanced endeavor of the former. In the *Evergetinos* we see the virtuous lives of the desert monks who, during the first few centuries of Christianity, fled to the barren deserts around the Mediterranean and lived the most extreme and awe-inspiring lives of asceticism in a search for God.

The Fathers (and among the Fathers, we include the spiritual Mothers) who dwelled in the desert and whose lives fill the *Evergetinos* are much like the sacred icons of the Orthodox Church. By naturalistic standards, they are distorted, strange, and foreign to us, images at times seemingly appropriate to the fanciful. Nevertheless, just as icons draw us into their spiritual auras and become windows through which we see faint glimpses of the heavenly world, so the Fathers of the desert draw us into the sphere of their spiritual power and force us deep into the recesses of our consciences and allow us to look on the almost-lost spiritual powers dwelling unheeded within ourselves. Their asceticism cannot be – perhaps *should not* be – imitated by many. They are simply a standard to which we should strive, a flame so bright as to kindle within us the spark of spiritual desire. But this is not to say that they are removed from us.

The desert Fathers speak of sexual desire, envy, greed, jealousy, hate, and the most complex human foibles. They expose to us what is all too familiar and obvious. They let us see with alarming clarity the depth of our depravity and the labyrinths of our sinful inner chasms. And though we probably cannot attain to the fullest extent the virtues by which these holy hermits overcame human depravity, we can see clearly the folly of a modern world seeking goodness, truth, purity, and virtue without first humbling itself before its Creator and the subtle inward world of spiritual truth. Hearing today of virtues, the ancient Fathers show them, by their examples, to be plastic virtues. Seeing today monuments of faith built with stone and mortar, the desert dwellers show us monuments of faith built on flesh and blood.

As we enter into the world of beginning monks, freshly having left the world, and accomplished elders who have gained discernment of the inner life, spiritual discretion, the ability to see into the hearts and minds of others, we embark on a journey into a strangely real world. In the small communities of monks gathered in the wilderness (*sketes*), we find those who, in their lives and by their experience, vivify the rules and commandments of Christian conduct. We see the living source of the rules which most Christians today emptily follow. And we see the mystical rewards and products of virtuous lives in these examples of perfection attained on earth. Indeed, we have an elemental encounter with what the Orthodox Christian life encompasses: a set of beliefs and practices gleaned from experience and a profound way of life, not a system based on regimented acts coldly governed by abstract beliefs and rules propped up with mere emotionalism. We touch what gives our otherwise vain and fruitless efforts in the Christian life their meaning and content. Standing before us is the answer to modern disbelief: the possibility of deeper life and the fulfillment of lost goals which, at least in the wild attempts by many contemporary religious groups to give external meaning to an internally moribund Christianity, have become meaningless, if not ignominious, pursuits.

The *Evergetinos* was first published in the eighteenth century through the efforts of Saint Makarios of Corinth and Saint Nikodemos of the Holy Mountain. It was thus taken from the hands of the monks of Mount Athos and made available to the Orthodox faithful. In addition to recent, excellent editions published in Greece, parts of the *Evergetinos* have appeared in English. However, these English translations have not adequately provided for the spiritual needs of Orthodox in the West. There are two reasons for this. Firstly, the writings in the *Evergetinos*, as we have observed, though not as advanced as those in the *Philokalia*, still express some very profound philosophical and psychological precepts. They are written in an ironic tone, often having shades and levels of meaning not immediately apparent. Moreover, since they are written largely for those seriously engaged in the spiritual struggle, they often assume some ascetic experience on the part of the reader.

Therefore, selections from the *Evergetinos* designed for the general reader should be made by those with spiritual experience and the discernment to know what is and what is not too complex for the beginner. This has not, in general, been the case. For the most part, the available translations are by Roman Catholics working from Latin texts with anecdotes that relate to an Eastern monasticism foreign to the traditions and development of Western monasticism, or by scholars with largely academic interest in the desert Fathers. However noble the efforts of these translators may be, they lack the very experience which the *Evergetinos* transmits and which is necessary in order to produce a useful introduction to Orthodox spirituality for the beginner or lay reader.

Secondly, there are today very few individuals who truly understand what translation is. I have noted that the presentation of deep spiritual writings demands very careful selection of passages by spiritually experienced individuals. How much more, then, we should expect such experience to play a role in the translation of the passages. Too many times we find that translators have fallen into a supercilious style of translation in which they unwittingly lose the meaning of a passage in their misguided efforts to show technical precision and, one might suspect, to demonstrate their superior knowledge of some language. They produce lengthy introductions in criticism of one or another translator, thereby, in the case of spiritual writings, acting against the very charity embodied in what they translate.

Even in the case of some superb translations, such as the translation of the *Philokalia* now in progress with the aid of such superior translators as Archimandrite Kallistos Ware and Professor Constantine Cavarnos, the publishers often show a complete lack of spiritual sensitivity. Certainly against the better judgment of Dr. Cavarnos (and no doubt other translators), the first volume of this project violated the arrangement of the writings made by Saint Nikodemos of the Holy Mountain, the first publisher of the *Philokalia*. In the interest of supposed "scholarly objectivity," the writings of Saint Anthony the Great were appended to the text with effusive accusations against their authenticity. An acquiescence to the spiritual authority of Saint Nikodemos, natural for anyone of spiritual knowledge, would have been the proper course. It would have reflected the understanding which is absolutely necessary for the preparation of spiritual books.

Thus it is that I offer the present slim volume of selections from the *Evergetinos*. They are not meant as pedantic considerations of the Greek text, but as comparative translations which bring out the simple messages of the easier lessons of the desert Fathers. They are meant as beginnings for beginners. The passages are translated primarily from the demotic Greek, the colloquial dialect of Greece, and therefore reflect the same concise, simplified versions which the less-sophisticated and less-learned (albeit, perhaps more pious) faithful of Greece have received. Some will find this offensive, since in places phrases and expressions, magnificently expressed in the better Greek dialect, but difficult to understand and confusing to the beginner, have been omitted. Still in other places, though as seldom as possible, the modern Greek renderings have been supplemented by phrases from the standard *Evergetinos* to insure clarity of meaning. Where extant English translations of the passages seem to express better the spiritual intent of the text, despite some disloyalty to the demotic Greek version, they have been incorporated into the final rendering.

There is, then, nothing precisely scholarly in what I have done. The concern has been for the transmission of certain spiritual precepts and for the selection of passages which are as beneficial to the layman as they are to the experienced monk. But even in this, a few words have to be said about the underlying theology of the desert Fathers and about their spiritual psychology. Let us take several important examples. It is almost impossible to capture in translation the Greek words *diakrisis* and *penthos*. The former word implies discretion, discernment, and even a supernatural kind of cognition. So when a monk possessed of spiritual *diakrisis* appears in the proverbs of the Fathers, I have arbitrarily called him a monk of discretion or a monk endowed with discernment. In the case of the latter word, one can render it grief, mourning, lamentation, and even, at times, something akin to repentance. I have tried not to be arbitrary in translating this word. In both cases it would be foolish to try, in the simple translation of a word, to convey the characteristics of an accomplished monk. *Diakrisis* and *penthos* have technical meanings in Orthodox patristic writings. If one can be somewhat arbitrary with the one and not with the other, this allowance can only result from some familiarity with the theology of those writings. For this reason I strongly suggest that the reader acquaint himself with Professor Constantine Cavarnos' essay, "The Philokalia," which constitutes the fourth chapter of his readable and essential book, *Byzantine Thought and Art* (Belmont, Mass., 1968). In a few pages one can gain an understanding of the spiritual terminology of the Fathers and enhance greatly his comprehension of their writing and deeds.

I must say, also, something about my style of translation. Demotic is, as it were, a short-hand version of the "pure" Greek dialect. This has necessitated, for clear understanding in the English text, some changes in the verb tenses and in the sequence of adjectival expressions. As well,I have taken the liberty of repeating nouns in some clauses where references are made by Greek pronouns having no counterparts in English. In the case of particularly complex or ironic statements, sometimes rendered idiomatically in the Greek, I have used an underlining purely of my own invention. In addition, I have felt free to include some idiosyncratic uses. While names are usually transliterated directly from the Greek (according to the modern rule) even when English translations are available (*e.g.*, "Antonios" instead of "Anthony," or "Markos" instead of "Mark"), in some cases I did not find this comfortable; hence, Abba "Moses" the Black. Further, I have used the word "Abba" much as we use today the word "Father." At times I have arbitrarily interchanged the words. And finally, the Greek word *"hosios"* I have translated as "holy" in most places, though, in order to enhance the text, as "Saint" in others. Otherwise, I have usually rendered the word *"hagios"* as

"Saint" (except when used as an adjective). I apologize for these oddities.

Now, lest anyone think that I have proceeded with an overestimation of my own abilities, may I add a crucial disclaimer? The following passages, by virtue of being translated from a demotic Greek version of the writings of the desert Fathers, aim at giving a simple and very understandable introduction to Orthodox spirituality. Moreover, they are comprised of selections which provide a deliberate and balanced view of the inner life of the desert dwellers. These two qualities, we have said, are the earmarks of a good translator and a good spiritual guide. I am neither. In no sense do I pretend to have adequate abilities to translate the sublime spiritual words of the Fathers. Nor, as is well known to those around me, am I a man of any spiritual attainment whatever. I have, rather, followed very closely and used as my primary original source a small volume, the *Mikros* (*"Small"* or *"Shorter"*) *Evergetinos* (Hagion Oros—Athens, 1977), by the monk Kallinikos of the Skete of Saint Ann on Mount Athos. In following his selections, I have necessarily benefited from the wisdom of Father Kallinikos. Whatever I have presented that is good is his; the errors and the poorness in presentation are my own.

I have taken a final liberty in this small effort. Combined with the anecdotes of the desert Fathers are a few anecdotes which I have attributed to spiritual people of our own times, mostly holy men and women living in Greece. I have done this to emphasize that, despite the waning tide of Orthodox spirituality today, there are still some spiritual Fathers of the stature of the ancients. The desert exists not just in the past years; it is also in our hearts. And though they are few and silent and hidden, there are today Fathers and Mothers dwelling in the deserts of their hearts. To the extent that we, too, search our hearts and turn to the inner life, God will no doubt raise up these men and cure, with their perfect examples, the spiritual malaise of our age. Then they can do with deeds what poor spiritual pariahs such as myself can only ape with limited offerings such as the present little book.

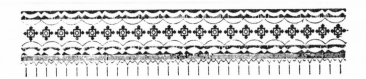

SECTION 1

Abba Antonios said: "The time is coming when people will be seized by manias and will behave like madmen. And if they see anyone acting reasonably, they will rise up against him saying: 'You are insane.' And they will have accurately said this to him, for he will not be like them."

* * *

Several brothers went to Abba Antonios to relate to him certain visions which they beheld and to ascertain from him whether the visions were true or of demonic origin. They had along with them a small donkey which died on the way. Just as they reached Abba Antonios, he, expecting them, said: "How did the little donkey die on the road?"

"How did you know this, Abba?" they said to him.

"The demons revealed it to me."

And they answered him: "It is for this reason that we came to see you, for fear of being deceived, since we see visions and many times they come true."

Thus, with the foregoing example of the donkey, the elder made it known to them that their visions came forth from the demons.

* * *

The same Abba Antonios, pondering the ways of God, once asked: "Lord, how does it happen that many live very few years and yet others reach a ripe old age? And how is it that some live in poverty while others are rich? And how is it that the unjust continue to grow richer and the just are poor?'' Then he heard a voice say to him: "Antonios, watch yourself, for those things which you ask about belong to the inscrutable ways of God's wisdom and it is not to your benefit to learn of them.''

* * *

Once Abba Antonios received a letter from Emperor Constantine the Great which requested him to go to Constantinople. He wondered about what to do. So he said to his disciple, Abba Paul: "What do you say? Should I go?'' And the Abba answered him: "If you go, you will be called 'Antonios'; however, if you do not go, 'Abba Antonios.'''

* * *

Once Abba Arsenios revealed his thoughts to an Egyptian elder and asked him about them. But a certain other Abba saw him and said to him: "Abba Arsenios, you have had so much education in Greek and Latin, yet you ask this man, so unlettered in worldly knowledge, about your thoughts?''

Abba Arsenios said to him: "Indeed, I know Roman and Greek letters well; but I have not yet learned even the alphabet of this simple man.''

* * *

A young monk sadly said the following to the holy Poimen: "My body, Abba, has been weakened by ascetic practices, but my passions do not yield.''

"The passions, my child,'' answered the wise Father, "are similar to tough thorns; in uprooting them, your hands of necessity bleed.''

* * *

"What am I to do, Abba, since passions and demons beset me?" a young monk asked the holy Sisoes.

"Do not say that you are bothered by demons, child," answered the elder, "because the greater part of us are beset by our own evil desires."

* * *

While still a neophyte in monastic life, Moses the Black (the Ethiopian) was warring against carnal desire. So he went, in a state of turbulence, to confess to Abba Isidoros.

The elder listened to him sympathetically and, when he had given him words of appropriate counsel, told him to return to his cell. However, inasmuch as Abba Moses was still hesitant, for fear of the flame of evil desires rekindling during his return, Abba Isidoros took him by the hand and led him to a small roof atop his cell.

"Look here," he told him, directing him towards the West. Thereupon Moses saw an entire army of wicked spirits with drawn bows, ready for warfare, and was terrified.

"Look towards the East now," the elder told him once more. Myriads of angels in military formation were standing ready to confront the enemy.

"All of these," Abba Isidoros told him, "are assigned by God to help the struggler. Do you see how our defenders are many more and incomparably stronger than our enemies?"

Moses thanked God with his heart for this revelation and, taking courage, returned to his cell to continue his struggle.

* * *

Abba John the Short, advising the young brothers to love fasting, told them frequently: "The good soldier, undertaking to capture a strongly fortified, enemy city, blockades food and water. In this way the resistance of the enemy is weakened and he finally surrenders. Something similar happens with carnal impulses, which severely war against a person in his youth. Blessed fasting subdues the passions and the demons and ultimately removes them far from the combatant."

"And the powerful lion," he told them another time, "frequently falls into a snare because of his gluttony, and all of his strength and might disappear."

* * *

"If Nabuzardan, the court cook of the King of the Babylonians, had not gone to Jerusalem, then the Temple would not have burned (cf. 2 Kings 24)," said Abba Poimen. "That is to say, a person's mind is not attacked by the flames of carnal pleasures, if a person is not conquered by gluttony."

* * *

Once a demonized youth went to the skete of some Fathers in order to be cured by their prayers. Out of humility, however, they fled. For much time, the unfortunate man suffered thus, until a certain elder took pity on him, crossed him with a wooden cross he had on his belt, and cast out the evil spirit.

"Since you evict me from my abode," the spirit said, "I will enter you."

"Come," the elder courageously answered him.

So it is that the demon entered into him and tortured him for a full twelve years. The holy one endured the struggle with fortitude, but fought against his enemy with superhuman fasting and unceasing prayer. All of those years he never even once put food in his mouth, chewing rather a few date pits every evening and swallowing only the juice from them.

Finally, conquered by the incessant struggle of the elder, the demon freed him.

"Why are you leaving?" the elder asker him. "No one is casting you out."

"Your fasting destroyed me," answered the demon, becoming invisible.

* * *

"My brother, if your soul were pure and upright before the Lord, you would be able to profit from all things of this life. If you were to see a wandering peddler, you would say to yourself: 'my soul, from the desire to earn fleeting, earthly goods, the peddler toils a great deal and endures much, concentrating on things which will not ultimately remain under his domain. Why, then, do you not look after those things which are eternal and incorruptible?' Once again, if you were to see those who dispute in court over financial matters, you would say: 'My soul, these people, often having not a single need, show such ardor and quarrel with such shouting between themselves. You, who owe to God a myriad of talents, why do you not implore God, bowing down as one should, to obtain cancellation of *that* debt?'

"If you were to see a builder making houses, you would again say: 'my soul, these same, even if they build houses from mud, show such great zeal to finish the work they have laid out. You, why are you indifferent to eternal structures and why do you not struggle to erect the abode of God within the soul, forming and joining the virtues by the will?'

"Now, in order not to be prolix in citing various circumstances one by one, let us say that we must take care to transform our worldly thoughts and observations, which are born of our material perspective on things of the present life, to spiritual ones. Thereby, we shall profit from all things with the help and assistance of Divine Grace" (Saint Ephraim).

* * *

"I burn with the passion to be martyred for the love of Christ," a neophyte monk one day said to an experienced elder.

"If you gladly take up your brother's burden at a time of temptation," the elder answered him, "it is like being thrown into the furnace with the three Holy Children."

* * *

"When I was a child," the Holy Makarios once said, "I

grazed cattle along with other children. One day they went to steal figs and took me along. When we returned to the herd, one of the figs fell from their basket and I picked it up and ate it. Even now that my hair has grown white, I remember that sin and I lament.''

* * *

"In case we should ever fall into carnal sin," Abba Moses told his disciples, "let us repent and let us mourn now before the lamentation of our dread condemnation prevents us."

* * *

Yet another time he said: "The virtues are born with tears and through them forgiveness is given. But when we cry, we must not raise the voice of our groaning in order to be heard by others. Let not our left hand, that is, our vanity, know what our right hand, the sorrow of the heart, does."

* * *

To a certain brother, who asked what to do when he had temptations or evil thoughts in his mind, the same elder answered:"Run, weeping, to the goodness of God, crying out with all of the power of your soul, asking aid. God is near to one who appeals to Him, the Holy Scriptures tell us."

* * *

When you feel compunction in your heart," a certain elder counsels, "leave all other thoughts and say to your mind: 'Perhaps the hour of my death is approaching and God is sending me mourning and tears in order to save me.' For since the devil wars more strongly against a man at the last, in order to root him in evil, so God sends him such things within, in order to save him."

* * *

"Man's conscience is like a spring," the Fathers say, "which, the deeper you hollow it out, the more greatly you cleanse it. If, however, you cover it with soil, in little time it will be lost."

* * *

At the moment that a holy elder was in the throes of death, the devil appeared before him and shouted at him: "You destroyed me, you wretch."

"I am still not sure of that, " the Saint replied, and reposed.

* * *

When he was about to die, the holy Agathon remained in his bed motionless for three days, his eyes open and upturned towards heaven. On the third day, when he recovered some, his disciples, who had assembled around him, asked him to tell them where his soul was during all of that interval of time.

"Before the judgement of God," he murmured, trembling.

"And you are afraid, Father?" the brothers asked with perplexity.

"I tried, as best I could, to keep the laws of God all of my life. But I am a man. How do I know that I have pleased God?" the holy one responded with great pain.

"You are not sure that your works were pleasing to God?" said the astonished monks.

"Until I am before God, no," answered the holy one, "for man judges with one standard and God with another."

The brothers wanted to ask other things for the benefit of their souls, but the holy one nodded to them not to speak any further.

"I am preoccupied," his lips whispered.

His countenance began to shine! His disciples saw him leave this vain world for eternal life with the joy which one feels when he sets off to meet his most beloved acquaintance.

* * *

"The good Christian," says the wise Abba Nistheros, "must take account of himself morning and evening and say: 'What, from all that God desires, did I do, and what did I neglect to do?' Only in this manner will one succeed in conducting himself in accordance with the will of God."

* * *

An elder went to visit Abba Achillas and saw him spitting blood from his mouth.

"What happened, brother," he asked.

And this man of forbearance replied. "What you saw was the word of a brother who shortly ago upset me. I struggled with difficulty not to answer him and I asked God to take the bitterness from my soul. And see how his word became blood in my mouth. Spitting, I cast out *with* it the affliction in my heart."

* * *

The holy Theodora was in the habit of telling her disciples very frequently how neither great asceticism, nor extremely hard work, nor any other sufferings whatsoever can save a man as much as true humility of the heart. She also related the following anecdote:

A certain hermit had a gift from God to cast out evil spirits. One time he asked to learn what they feared most and what compelled them to flee.

"Perhaps it is fasting?" he asked one of them.

"We," the evil spirit replied, "neither ever eat nor ever drink."

"Sleepless vigils, then?"

"We do not sleep at all."

"Flight from the world?"

"Supposedly an important thing. But we spend the greater part of our time wandering around the deserts."

"I implore you to confess what it is that can subdue you," insisted the elder.

The evil spirit, compelled by a supernatural force, was

pressed to answer: "Humility—which we can never overcome."

* * *

"The blacksmith, who pounds a piece of iron," says Saint Antonios the Great, "has previously thought about what he wants to make—a sickle, a knife, an axe—, and works accordingly. And so let the man of God ponder in advance which virtue he wishes to acquire, in order not to toil aimlessly."

* * *

"All excesses," said another Father, "are products of the devil."

* * *

Two fellow ascetics struggled in the Thebaid desert. But they were young and inexperienced and the devil set a great many snares for them.

The younger one once was warring fervently against the flesh. It was thus that he lost his composure and patience and said resolutely to the older ascetic: "I cannot endure any longer; I am going to return to the world."

The older one, terribly distraught by the temptation which had befallen his brother, tried to constrain him.

"I will not let you leave here, to waste your efforts and to lose your purity."

But there was no convincing him!

"I am not staying," he said. "I am leaving. I will taste of everything and then we will see. If you want, come with me and we will either both return, or I will stay forever in the world."

The older brother, not knowing what to do, went to seek counsel from an elder who was their neighbor.

"Go with him," he told him after he had heard of the situation. "I do not think that God, for the sake of your efforts, will let him be lost."

And so the two fellow ascetics set off together to go down into the city. But just as they got near, the one who had been tempted suddenly said to his brother: "Suppose I were to fulfill my desire. What would I gain by it? Come, my brother, let us return to our solitude."

The older brother looked at him with confusion and could not believe his ears. Then he remembered the words of the holy elder: "God will see your efforts and will not let him come to harm."

And, indeed, the brother was relieved from his powerful battle and the two returned happily to their cells.

* * *

Abba Markos once asked the holy Arsenios why it is that the most pious and virtuous people pass through the world with numerous sorrows and in privation.

"Sorrows, for those who accept them with forbearance," the holy one answered, "are the salt which prevents putrefaction by sins and allows the soul to approach heaven cleansed."

* * *

It is said by the Fathers of Abba John the Persian that malefactors once went into his hut with the apparent intent of killing him. The blessed one prepared a basin and stooped down to wash their feet, as he would do for his best friends. At this, the malefactors, embarrassed, left him alone and departed.

* * *

One night thieves went to a certain hermit.

"We came to take your things," they said to him viciously.

Without losing composure, he said to them, "Come in and take whatever you like."

They emptied his poor hut of every last thing and left hurriedly. They forgot, however, to take a small flask that was hanging from a beam of the roof. The hermit took it down and, running behind the robbers, shouted for them to listen and to stop.

"Come back, brothers, to take this too." And he showed them from afar the small flask.

They were amazed by his forgiving nature and returned, not to take the flask, but to offer repentance and to return all of his things.

"This is, indeed, a man of God," they said among themselves.

* * *

"If our prayer is not in harmony with our deeds, we labor in vain," Abba Moses often told the young monks.

"How are we to accomplish such harmony?" they asked him one day.

"When we make that which we seek fitting to our prayer," explained the saint. "Only then can the soul be reconciled with its Creator and its prayer be acceptable, when it sets aside all of its own evil intentions."

* * *

And the very wise Abba Agathon said: "When I see that a person—even if he is very dear to me—is becoming the occasion for me to acquire some fault, I immediately cut off all ties with him."

* * *

"If you wish to progress in what is good," said another Father, "do not associate with a person of ill will."

* * *

A novice monk sought out the advice of a certain elder of discretion: "If the behavior of one of my brothers scandalizes me, should I ask his forgiveness?"

"Ask his forgiveness," the elder answered, "but cease associating with him. Have you not heard what Arsenios the Great advises? 'Have love for all, but be detached from everyone.' "

* * *

"If a man does not say with his heart, 'only God and I exist in this world,' he finds no peace," said Abba Alonios.

* * *

"Beware, Christian, never to wrong your brother, lest your prayer become unacceptable before God. If, nevertheless, you wrong someone, your prayer is not acceptable. The sighs of the one wronged do not allow it to reach heaven. If you learn that someone is speaking ill things of you and he should come at some time to visit you, do not show him in your mannerisms that you know of all this and that you are upset with him. Appear to him cheerful, with a calm face and a sweet way, so that your prayer might be bold before God," a certain Abba advises.

* * *

And see what Abba Moses says of prayer: "Take care to maintain deep in your heart cognizance of your sinful state, that your prayer might be acceptable. When you occupy your mind with your own sins, you will not have time to keep track of the faults of others."

* * *

"Do you wish God to hear your prayer immediately, brother?" asks Abba Zenon. "When you lift your hands up to heaven, pray first of all, with your heart, for your enemies and God will grant you speedily whatever else you request."

* * *

Then there was a woman who was suffering from cancer and, having heard of the reputation of Abba Longinos, decided to find him that he might restore her health. While she was looking for him here and there in the desert, she encountered an elderly monk cutting wood. She approached him and asked him where Abba Longinos stayed.

"What do you want with him?" the monk asked. "I advise you not to go to him because he is not a good man....But maybe something is troubling you?"

The unfortunate woman then showed him an open sore which gave off an unbearable odor. The monk made the sign of the cross over her and told her: "Return to your home and God will heal you. Longinos cannot help you in anything."

She left, receiving the words of the unknown monk with faith. By the time she reached her home, not a trace of her fearful illness remained. She later learned from the other brothers that the one who made her well in this strange way was Abba Longinos himself.

* * *

A young monk asked Abba Moses to give him a piece of useful advice.

"Stay in your cell and your cell will teach you," the wise elder answered.

* * *

"It is impossible for a monk to have Christ continuously in his heart without silence, humility, and unceasing prayer," the same elder used to say.

* * *

Once the holy Makarios went to keep an ill hermit company. Casting an eye around the ill man's naked cell, he saw that there was nowhere even a scrap of food.

"What would you like to eat, brother?" asked the Saint.

The ill monk hesitated to answer. What was he supposed to ask for, since there was nothing in that wilderness? Finally, since the Saint was waiting for him to answer, he said that he had the desire for a little soup made with flour. But where was flour to be found?

The holy Makarios, so as to comfort his sick brother, went

fifty miles on foot to Alexandria to find flour.

* * *

In the present time, a struggling Father went to a bishop of discernment and told him of a spiritual problem. It seems that the Father was so struck by spiritual words and Divine Services that he could not control the flow of tears from his eyes. Embarrassed by this phenomenon when it took place in the presence of others, the monk found it increasingly difficult to participate in public worship.

The wise bishop advised the Father that he was suffering from hidden pride and that the most efficacious tears spiritually were those hidden within the heart. The Father wrestled endlessly with the secret pride within him, sincerely asking for God's help, and his tears began to subside.

* * *

SECTION 2

A highly respected elder of our own days was visited by a young man tempted with lustful desires. Questioning the man about the sincerity of his intent to overcome such temptation, the elder asked him if he was willing to obey without question the advice he was about to be offered.

"I will do whatever you say," the man answered.

The elder then advised him to take a certain bus to its last stop, get off the bus, and remove all of his clothes within sight of the bystanders there. With great hesitation, but nevertheless acting out of sincere obedience, the young man went to wait for the bus that he was instructed to take.

In the meantime, the wise elder sent a brother to fetch the waiting man, explaining to him that the elder wished to speak with him once more before he boarded the bus. When the young man again approached the elder, the elder asked him: "Do you still have your lustful thoughts?"

The formerly tempted man answered, "No, Father, they have left me."

* * *

Once I saw the devil lying in wait outside the cell of my disciple," said a sagacious elder. "So I cast an eye inside to see what my disciple was doing. He had the Holy Scriptures open in front of him and was plunged deep in study. As soon as he closed the book and ended his reading, the devil rushed in to tempt him.

* * *

"The sacred writers of the Old and New Testaments, with the inspiration of the Holy Spirit, authored books," said a certain elder. "The Fathers took care to apply the writings in their lives. The next generation knew them by heart. But those of modern times have copied them and shut them away in libraries."

* * *

"Come, my child, and taste of the blessed life of obedience," Abba Moses told a young man who was ready to follow the monastic life. "In this life, you will find humility, strength, joy, patience, and forbearance. Within it, contrition is born and love blossoms. It aids the good monastic disciple to keep all of the divine commandments throughout his life."

* * *

Likewise, Abba Iperechios calls obedience the invaluable treasure of the monk: "Let him who has attained it be assured that his prayer will always be heard and will be presented with boldness at the altar of Him Who was obedient even unto death."

* * *

Again, Abba Rouphos says that greater glory awaits the monk who is obedient to an elder than the hermit who lives by his own will in the solitude of the desert.

* * *

"There are three things especially pleasing to God," said Abba Joseph the Thebite. "Illnesses suffered with patience, works done without ostentation and for *His* love only, and submission to a spiritual elder with perfect self-denial. This last thing will gain the greatest crown."

* * *

Once some elders went to visit Abba Antonios. Along with them was Abba Joseph. The Great Father, to test them, chose a certain written maxim and asked each of them, one by one, to tell its meaning. So each one began to explain it according to his understanding

"You did not find its meaning," he answered each of them. Then came Abba Joseph's turn.

"What do you have to say about this, Joseph?" Antonios the Great asked him.

"I do not know of such things," he replied.

"Abba Joseph gave the correct answer," the holy one then said, marvelling at Abba Joseph's humility.

* * *

The Fathers of the skete once gathered to speak among themselves about spiritual things, and forgot to invite Abba Kopris. They began to discuss the person of Melchizidek and did not come to agreement in their opinions. Then they remembered Abba Kopris and sent summons to him so that they could get his opinion. When he heard of the cause of their disagreement and the subject about which they had idled away so many hours arguing, he struck himself three times on the mouth and said: "Woe to you, monk. You have set aside that which God has asked of you and you have sought to find those things which He will never ask of you."

Hearing his wise words, the other elders left their gathering and returned to their cells, pensive.

* * *

"Whosoever enters a perfume shop," a certain elder related, "even if he does not purchase any perfume, leaves filled with fragrance. The same thing happens to one who associates with holy people. He takes on himself the spiritual aroma of their virtue."

* * *

THE ANCIENT FATHERS OF THE DESERT

"If a person desires, he may attain holiness as much at the setting of the sun as at its dawning," Antonios the Great said, teaching his disciples thereby the power of repentance.

* * *

Three elders customarily went three times a year to the mountain of Abba Antonios to be taught by the Great Saint. Two of them would ask various questions concerning spiritual and bodily exercises. In this way they provided the occasion for the Saint to pour forth the river of wisdom flowing within him. The third elder always listened silently, without asking anything. Once the Saint asked him: "So many years you have visited me, brother, without making the slightest inquiry. Do you not wish to learn anything?"

"It is enough for me to see you, Abba. Indeed, this has taught me much," the elder answered reverently.

* * *

"For someone to teach another, he must be healthy in his soul and free of passions," says Abba Poimen. "There is no use in building the house of another, your own being destroyed."

"He who teaches others, without putting to practice any of that which he teaches," the same Father further says, "is like a spring which irrigates and flows over all that is around it, while it is filled with every sort of dirt."

* * *

"Truly wise," said Abba Iperechios, "is he who teaches, not with words, but with deeds."

Another wise Father compares one who teaches only with words, without doing works, with trees which have leaves, but bear no fruit.

One of the great Fathers of the desert told a certain elder, his neighbor, who always accepted visitors and taught them: "Be careful, brother, for while the oil lamp indeed gives light to many, its wick holder is usually burned."

* * *

"He who knows himself is a man," said Abba Poimen.

* * *

A desert elder set off for the nearest village to sell his baskets. On the road that he was going down, the devil found him and, out of the intense malice he had toward the elder, snatched the baskets from his hands and disappeared. The elder, without being at all upset, raised his eyes to heaven and said, "I thank you, my God, that you have relieved me of my burden and the trouble of going down to the village." Then the devil, not suffering the calmness of the hermit, threw the baskets in his face, shouting: "Take them back, old man."

The monk gathered them up again and continued on his way to the village.

* * *

"I once saw all of the snares of the devil spread out across the earth," said the Great Antonios, "and I became terrified."

"Is it possible that anyone can escape them?" he said, sighing.

He then heard a mysterious voice answering him: "He who is humble of mind."

* * *

While still a young monk, Abba Poimen asked to learn from Antonios the Great what he should do to find his salvation.

"Acknowledge your faults with a broken heart," this Father of Fathers answered, "and humble yourself before God. Also, endure patiently the temptations which occur to you and be sure that you will be saved."

* * *

The fathers relate to us that, besides other divine gifts, there was also bestowed by God upon Saint Euthymios the following: to perceive, from the external appearance, the internal activities of the souls of people, as though seeing them in mirror images; and to know in detail the thoughts with which each one battled, and, indeed, which among these thoughts he was defeating and by which, through the operation of the devil, he was being defeated.

It is further said of him that sometimes he confided to certain brothers, who went to visit him on their own, that many times he would see angels plainly in front of him, liturgizing and drawing near the Holy Gifts. At the time of the communion of the Master's Body, he saw some of the communicants as though they were shining, while others darkened in appearance—namely those who were not worthy of that light and of the brightness of Holy Communion.

Thus taking the occasion of these supernatural visions, he warned the brothers against participation in the communion of the Divine Gifts without proper preparation, and counselled them excellently, relying on the Apostle, saying that every Christian should take care to examine himself with exactness to see if he is worthy, thereby, of communicating the Holy Bread and the Holy Chalice with shuddering fear.

The communicant—Euthymios the Great continually taught—must know well that whoever approaches unworthily to communicate "eats and drinks" censure and condemnation unto himself.

So if anyone has been overcome by rancor or hate or envy, by pride, abusiveness, obscenity in expression, or indecent desires, or is in any way taken by any other passion whatsoever, let him not participate in Divine Communion, if first he has not cleansed his soul from all of these noxious things through repentance. Because, as the spirit of God says through the Liturgist, the Holy Things are not fitting to those who are profane, but only to the holy.

To the extent, then, that you have a clean conscience and it inspires in you the boldness to approach the Lord, "draw near to Him and be enlightened by Him, being also certain that you will not be chastened."

* * *

The following is said of the holy Archbishop John of San Francisco, a great luminary of our times: "So virtuous was his life on earth, that even after death he suffered the calumny of others."

* * *

A contemporary monk advised his brothers thus: "If you do not live by principles, do not pretend to adhere to them."

And again: "Today, when there is so little external monasticism, most monks must live within themselves. This means that there is no brother to admonish you or to be your example. You must admonish yourself and set an example for yourself. All of the goals, all of the rewards, and all of the standards have become internal. And while this may seem tragic, it is probably merciful."

* * *

The blessed Synkletike related to the Sisters that, "those who begin the life in God encounter much toil and struggles in the beginning, afterwards, however, finding indescribable joy.

"For," she said, "just as those who wish to light a fire are at first choked by smoke and their eyes water from the fumes, yet later succeed at their task, so we who wish to light the divine fire within us must know that we will succeed at this only by many struggles and toil; for the Lord also says, 'I came to cast fire upon the earth, and what else do I wish if the fire be more greatly kindled?'

"Indeed some," the blessed one continues, "while tolerating the bother and hindrance of the smoke in order to do a little work at the beginning, nonetheless, out of laziness, did not light a fire; for they went away quickly and did not have the forbearance to persist to the end."

* * *

The same Amma said: "Many live in the wilderness and behave as though they were in a town. The latter are wasting their time. It is possible to be a hermit in the mind while living among the masses; likewise, it is possible to be a hermit and live in the crowd of one's own thoughts."

* * *

The holy woman further said: "While a person is in a monastery, obedience is preferred to ascetic practice. The former teaches humility, the latter teaches pride."

* * *

The daughter of a certain rich man in Alexandria was suddenly seized by a wicked spirit and was tormented severely. Her father spent much money in order to make her well. But fruitlessly. The condition of the young girl became worse all the time. Somehow the Father learned that a hermit, who lived alone up on a mountain, had the gift from God to cast out demons. He was told, however, that the hermit was so humble that he would never agree to perform such a cure. So the nobleman had to find some other pretext by which to get him to his home.

One day the hermit went down to the city to sell his baskets. The father of the girl sent a servant to buy some and to invite the hermit home to be paid. He unsuspectingly went. As soon as he set foot in the door, the demonized girl, who was hidden behind the door, rushed at him and gave him a hard slap across the face. The holy hermit, without losing his calm, turned his other cheek, thus carrying out the commandment of the Lord.

Then this surprising incident took place: the demonized girl began to quiver wildly and to utter despairing cries: "O, hurry! I must leave. I cannot stay any longer. The commandment of Christ is casting me out."

With those words, the tormented creature was set free. The whole family, along with the daughter, who had regained her rational powers, glorified God for the great miracle which they

had seen with their own eyes and looked for the holy elder so
they could thank him. He, however, fleeing from all human
praise, had totally disappeared.

When the Fathers in the desert were informed of these facts,
they said among themselves that nothing so puts down the pride
of the devil as humility and obedience to the divine commandments.

* * *

"He who has his mind under control when he prays, and is
careful in what he says, keeps away the demons," says Saint
Ephraim the Syrian. "He, however, who elevates himself is
duped."

* * *

God requires these three things, which were bestowed in Holy
Baptism, from every man: correct belief in his soul, truth on his
tongue, and moderation in his body.

* * *

A certain industrious monk, who struggled for virtue with all
of his powers, once weakened and fell into laziness. However,
he quickly recovered and said to himself: "You poor man. Since
when do you scorn your salvation? Do you not fear death and
judgment?" With such thoughts, he became more eager in
God's work.

One day, while he was praying, wicked spirits gathered
around him and tried hard to distract him from his prayer.

"Why are you tormenting me?" the brother said with ex-
asperation. "Was it not enough that you pulled me down into
sloth so many times?"

"When you were lazy, you did not give us the slightest trouble," the demons answered with malice, "and we ignored you.
Now that you oppose us, we battle you."

When the brother heard these things, he pushed himself all

the more in spiritual struggle and, with the grace of God, progressed in virtue.

* * *

A brother, who pointlessly passed his time neglecting his salvation, once went down to the city to sell his baskets. Evening fell while he was on his way, however, and so as not to be in danger in the dark night, he found improvised lodging in an old tomb. He lay down to rest and when, out of sleepiness, he was finally closing his eyes, he saw opposite him two demons scrutinizing him.

"Fancy that! Look there—that monk had the nerve to lie down on a grave," one of them said. "Let us vex him so that he has to leave our habitation."

"Let us not waste out time with *him*," the other demon answered contemptuously. "He belongs to us. He eats, drinks, gossips, neglects his duties, and serves us in almost all ways. Let us go tempt those who battle us day and night with their prayer and asceticism."

The brother, seeing that even the demons disregarded him, took control and became a good monk.

* * *

Saint Athanasios, when he found himself on the patriarchal throne of Alexandria, called Abba Pambo to go to the city on an ecclesiastical matter. The first person that the holy man met, on passing through the walls of the large city, was a woman dressed up so as to ensnare her victims. Seeing her, the elder became tearful.

"Why are you crying, Father?" the brother who was accompanying him asked.

"For two reasons," the elder answered, sighing. "First of all, for the loss of her soul, and then because I do not take as much care to please my Lord as she does to please licentious men."

* * *

And something similar happened to Bishop Nonos and Saint Pelagia, as her biographer relates to us.

Once the Patriarch of Antioch was sitting with his bishops in the courtyard of the church of Saint Julian. While they were engaged in discussion, they heard an unusual commotion in the street. At that moment a luxurious carriage was passing by outside the church. The courtesan Pelagia was pridefully seated inside. The road sparkled from the brilliance of the jewels which she wore. The air was filled with the scent of her expensive perfumes. The crowd of people cheered her as though they were out of their minds.

The bishops turned their heads aside in disgust, to avoid facing the satanic woman, who had led so many of the young aristocrats of the city into the mire of immorality. Only one, Bishop Nonos, followed her persistently with his gaze, until she disappeared at a turn in the road. Afterwards he turned to the other bishops and said to them with a sorrowful voice:

"Woe to us, brothers in Christ. This woman puts us to great shame. Did you see how much care she takes in dressing her body in order to lure her lovers? While we lazy people—what do we do to adorn our souls to attract the love of our heavenly Bridegroom?"

Saying these things, he prayed with fervor for that sinful soul. And his prayer was heard. Divine Grace restored her and Pelagia came to believe in Christ, repented her sinful life, was baptized by the holy Nonos, and came to a holy end.

* * *

A monk under obedience to a certain great elder also suffered from carnal desire and struggled hard without regard for his body. Seeing him struggle mercilessly, his elder felt sorry for him.

"Do you want me to ask God to deliver you from this torment, my child?" he asked him one day when he was especially sorrowful.

"No, Father," said the brave struggler. "For, though I am laboring severely, I see great benefit in my soul from the strug-

gle. Pray only that God will give me the strength to endure."
"Indeed, you are doing well, my child," the elder then told him with admiration, "and you surpass me."

* * *

"My unclean thoughts are about to kill me," a brother confessed to a certain elder.
"Do you know what mothers do when they want to wean their babies? They put a bitter substance on their breast. Likewise, put in your mind, instead of some bitter substance, the memory of death and eternal damnation and immediately you will cut off any unclean thought," the wise elder advised him.

* * *

A certain young monk, who struggled arduously to preserve the purity of his body and his soul, when he happened to be bothered by carnal desire, would say to the evil spirit with rage: "Go to the outer darkness. Can it be that you do not know that, even though I am unworthy, I bear parts of Christ within me?"
With these words he would cast out temptation, in the same way that one blows on a lighted oil lamp and immediately it goes out.

* * *

An elder gave this advice to a certain young man who asked him to tell him how to be saved: "Force yourself, my child, to do whatever the condemned do in prison. Hear them asking continually, with agony written on their faces: 'Where is the Governor? When is he coming? Maybe he has granted a pardon.' They tremble and cry, waiting for the moment when they will be led to the place of execution. Say in your mind, too: 'My sins have condemned me. How shall I face the righteous Judge? How will I defend myself?' Grieve and weep over your sins, so as to be saved."

* * *

For nine years a monk was tormented by the thought of leaving his monastery. Each evening he packed his clothes and said to himself: "I will leave tomorrow without delay."

When day would break, he would reflect: "For the love of Christ, I will be patient today and leave tomorrow."

Since he struggled arduously for eight whole years and was not overcome by his thoughts, the Lord took the temptation from him.

* * *

A monk found a great deal of temptation in the place where he first began to struggle. Once he lost his patience and decided to go far away to find his peace. Just as he stooped to tie his sandals, he saw someone in front of him tying his sandals, too.

"Who are you?" he asked him.

"The one who is pushing you out of here. And I am making ready to precede you to where you plan to take refuge."

It was the devil who had tried to push him out; but he did not succeed at it, because the brother stayed in his cell after that and struggled with patience, until he conquered his temptations.

* * *

"When wicked thoughts war with me," Abba John the Short said, "I do what a wayfarer would do if he were walking in the wilderness and suddenly saw a wild beast pursuing him: find a tree and climb up to the top to be saved. And so I flee to God with prayer and escape from the attack of wicked thoughts."

* * *

A monk of our day said: "One commandment could cure the ills of those who cause turmoil in the Church today: 'judge no one.' This should be the motto of those who hold firm to Orthodox tradition."

* * *

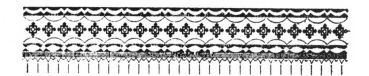

SECTION 3

A woman of sin once made up her mind, and wagered with her friends, that she could, without fail, succeed in leading into her nets a hermit, who lived on a mountain far from the city and about whom it was said by all that he was a holy man.

She wore a thick veil, which hid her attractiveness, and climbed the mountain. Her friends waited for her half-way up the road. As evening fell, she knocked at the door of the hermit's cave. He was disturbed when he saw her: "How can it be that a woman would be found at such an hour in this wilderness?"

"Ah, devil, this is one of your enticements," he mused.

He asked her who she was and what she was looking for. She turned on the tears.

"For hours on end I have been wandering in the wilderness, Father. I lost my way and my companions and I do not even know how I got here. But in the name of God, do not let the wild beasts eat me."

The hermit found himself in a dilemma. Should he take a woman into his living quarters? No such thing had ever occurred to him. But, on the other hand, should he let a creature of God be eaten by wild beasts? That would be inhuman, almost criminal. Finally, sympathy got the better of him and he took her in. She then took off her veil, supposedly ingenuously, and showed him her charms. Temptation began to inflame the desires of the combatant, since the act was no longer impeded.

He threw a few dry leaves on the ground and told the woman to lie down, while he removed himself to the depths of the cave. He kneeled and prayed fervently.

"Tonight," he reflected, "I have to wage the toughest battle against the visible and invisible enemy, and either I shall be victorious, or I will waste all of my labors."

As the night progressed, so much more the flame of his desire burned him. For one moment he felt his resistance yield and he was terrified.

"Those who defile their bodies with sinful acts go to hell," he said almost screaming. "And now to test to see if *you* will endure in the torturing fire."

He lighted his oil lamp and put his finger in the flame. But the other flame which burned his flesh was stronger and did not let him feel pain from the burn. Since his first finger had become useless, he put his second finger into the flame of the oil lamp, and then the third. By the time morning came, he had burned the five fingers of his hand.

That vile woman followed the superhuman struggle of the servant of God from a hidden vantage point and, seeing him obstinately burn all of his fingers, one after the other, was so shaken that she dropped dead of her terror.

Her friends, in the meantime, made a surprise incursion on the elder's cave in order to get a laugh at his expense. However, they found him outside in prayer.

"Did a woman perhaps show up here last evening?" they-asked him.

"She is inside sleeping," he answered them.

They went in and found her dead.

He then uncovered his hand and showed them his fingers.

"Do you see here what the daughter of the devil did to me?" The commandment of Christ, however, commands me to return good for evil."

He stood up and prayed over her soulless body and brought it back to life.

* * *

On the road one day, a young monk met some nuns, who were going down to the city. He immediately changed his course, in order to avoid greeting them. Their superior then stopped him and said: "You did well, brother, for your weakness. If you were, however, a perfect monk, you would not have perceived that we are women."

* * *

"My brother, take care with all of your heart, when you study the Divine Scriptures, to drink in avidly the richness which proceeds from your study, exactly as a baby drinks milk from the maternal breast. From the study of Divine Scripture, you will learn of the bright feats of virtue and thus your heart will be filled with joy and delight.

"If the interpreters of the writings of the wise of *this* world carefully study non-existent wisdom (for the wisdom of the-present world 'is foolishness before God'), with far *greater* enthusiasm *we* should study and learn by heart the words of God, for the salvation of our souls; and this the Holy Spirit lauds, blessing those who explore 'His testimonies,' because such as these will have sought God with all of their hearts.

"Is there anyone more perverted than he who has sweet and savory water and does not give a drink to his thirsty soul? Is there anyone more selfish than he who holds on to a beneficial book and does not give it to his brother to build him up spiritually? And can you imagine a lazier man than one who is thirsty and sits next to a well, not raising his hand to take water and satisfy his thirst? Is there a man more unprogressive and spiritually indifferent than the one who has, or receives, a religious book, yet does not care to read it?

"My brother, labor with anyone who asks you to teach him to read in order to study the wonders of God and to bless His majestic Name. And be certain that God will reward you for this labor" (Saint Ephraim).

* * *

"My brother, do you consider yourself spiritually learned? From your deeds you can perceive the actuality of this character trait; for, exactly as the body is dead without the breath, so any knowledge, without accompanying spiritual works, is dead and of no benefit. So if it is wrong for a Christian not to know Scripture, it is doubly wrong when he knows Scripture, but nevertheless disdains it by not applying its teachings to his life.''

* * *

"My brother, wisdom is not found in much learning and many letters; rather, as the Holy Scriptures say, 'the beginning of wisdom is the fear of the Lord, and prudence the desire of the Holy; indeed, it is good to know the law of the mind.' This is correct, for faith in God engenders a good mind, and the good mind is a river of living water; he who has attained it will be filled with its beneficial and life-bearing waters.

"Neither wisdom nor prudence can exist where there is not fear of the Lord, because the wealth of wisdom is to revere the Lord, to whom belongs all glory'' (Saint Ephraim).

* * *

A beginning monk, who went to a certain elder to confess, posed, among others, this question: "Why, Father, do I fall so often into sloth?"

"You lack the faith which makes you see God everywhere; for this reason you can be careless and lazy about your salvation,'' the discerning elder wisely explained.

* * *

The brothers of a certain skete gathered in a circle around one of the Fathers there to hear spiritual words from his mouth.

"Why is the soul not attracted by the promises of God, but more easily swept away by the deceptive things of the world?'' someone asked.

"Because it does not have faith,'' answered the elder. "When the soul, through faith, has tasted of *heavenly* good things, it is

* * *

impossible for it to be tempted by the vanity of the world.''

* * *

"The more that we bear continually in mind the difficulties which by chance our brothers might have brought upon us," said Saint Makarios, "the more we are removed by this from God. When we forget those difficulties immediately, the demons do not dare to tempt us.''

* * *

A brother who had quarreled with a certain other brother went to his neighbor, an elder, and confessed to him: "Such and such a brother, Father, greatly embittered me and the thought of seeking revenge plagues me.''

"Lock yourself in your cell, brother, and do not cease, day or night, to pray for him. Only in this way will you be released from the passion that seethes in you," the elder advised him.

The brother obeyed and, within one week, he found peace in his soul.

* * *

"If anyone abuses you," a certain Father says, "bless him. If he accepts the blessing, it is good for both of you. If, however, he does not accept it, you receive a blessing from God and the abuse rests on him.''

* * *

An inexperienced monk went in a distressed state to Abba Poimen: "I fell into great fault, Father," he confessed, "and I have tried for at least three years to repent.''

"That is a long time," the holy one told him.

"Are three *months* enough, then?''

"That, too, is a long time," answered the holy one. "I assure you that, if you sincerely repent and make a firm decision never to commit the same error, in three days you are received by God's goodness.''

* * *

Another brother asked the same elder whether God easily forgives the sins of man.

"How is it possible for Him not to forgive, my child, He Who teaches man forbearance? Did he not order Peter to forgive one who falls into error 'even seven times seventy,' that is, to infinity?" answered the holy elder.

* * *

Again, a certain other person asked him to explain to him exactly what repentance is.

"Not to repeat the same sins," responded Saint Poimen.

* * *

"If you wish to leave sinful desires and avoid foul language, do not act foolishly. Avoid the circumstances in which these weaknesses arise," advises a young monk of modern times.

* * *

A brother confessed to Abba Sisoes: "I fell, Father. What do I do now?"

"Get up," the holy elder told him, with his characteristic simplicity.

"I got up, Father, but I fell again into the cursed sin," the brother confessed grievingly.

"And what prevents you from getting up again?"

"Until when?" asked the brother.

"Until death finds you, whether standing or falling down. It is written, 'wherever I shall find you, there I will also judge you,' the elder explained. Just pray to God that you are found at your last moment standing upright in holy repentance."

* * *

From a modern struggler: "People who ask many questions and want many answers are fools. Distrusting themselves, they

turn to the vain and empty opinions of others."
Also: "To see perfection in oneself is the beginning of error."

* * *

A young monk confessed with soul-felt pain to one of the Fathers that his thoughts about returning to the world warred against him. "I purposelessly remain in the desert, Abba. I do nothing and surely I will not be saved."

The wise elder answered him: "But even if, my child, we do not anticipate stepping into the promised land, it is of greater benefit to leave our bones here on the desert, than to return to the bondage of Egypt."

* * *

A very devout and virtuous monk had a sister in the city, who lived a dissolute life and led many young men into sin. The brothers in the desert often urged the monk to go to the city to bring his straying sister to her senses. At first he hestitated. He feared the dangers hiding in the world for young monks. Afterwards, however, out of obedience, he decided to go.

Just as he got near his father's home, the neighbors saw him coming and informed his sister. The straying sister's heart jumped at this unexpected news. For years she had wanted to see her beloved brother. She gave leave of her companions and ran into the street to greet her brother just as she was to be found in her house, with bare feet and her head uncovered.

He, beholding her destitute state with his own eyes, was greatly troubled. His soul wept. "Are you not sorry for your soul, my sister," he told her sorrowfully, "and for those who, on your account, go astray? Think of what awaits you after death!"

The innocent face of the brother, his unassuming attitude, the tears of compassion that flowed from his eyes, along with his just admonition, shook the sinful woman.

"Is there salvation even for me?" her lips murmured.

"O yes, if you sincerely desire it enough."

"Take me with you," she begged, "and do not leave me by myself to struggle with the fierce billows of sin."

"Put on your sandals, cover your head, and follow me," the monk said resolutely.

"But let me go as I am, brother, because, if I go back into this workshop of Satan, who knows if I will have the strength to come back out?"

The monk was pleased with her firm resolve. Without wasting time, he led her out of the city and they went on their way to the desert. He intended to take her to a convent that was known to him. While they were walking, they saw a caravan in the distance, coming to where they were.

"Get out of sight a little, sister," the monk told her. "Hide behind the bushes; for these people, not knowing you are my sister, might see us together and be scandalized."

She complied with his advice. When the caravan passed, the brother yelled to her to continue on their way. She did not seem to hear. The monk went near and talked to her again. He pushed her with his foot. There did not appear to be any sign of life. She had died. He saw her bare feet completely covered with blood and torn to pieces by the stones on the road.

Disconsolate over the sudden death of his sister, the monk returned to his cell. Uncertainty ate away at him.

"It is impossible for her to be saved," his mind told him, "since she did not have time to repent."

He related in every detail all that happened to the elders in the desert. They ordered a fast and prayers for her soul. It was then revealed to a very holy hermit that God had accepted the repentance of the sinful woman and had enlisted her among the righteous for the self-denial she showed, as well as for reviling, not only material things, but her own body.

* * *

A spiritual man living in our times said: "Our spiritual Fathers are mostly books. This has a disadvantage, in that we never see flesh-and-blood spiritual guides. It has an advantage, in that flesh and blood guides sometimes die. Books do not.

"Moreover, while especially holy men do not abandon us when they repose, our impurity prevents us from seeing them with our own eyes. But even our impurity cannot prevent us from seeing what they have written in books."

* * *

Heed what we read in the "*Asketika*" of the great teacher and ascetic, Saint Isaak the Syrian: "By the same means that one lost goodness, he must try to acquire it again. Do you owe a debt of gold to God? He does not want pearls from you. Have you lost your prudence? He does not ask of you acts of charity, but requires sanctification of your body. Have you scorned the commandment of love, being conquered by the passion of envy? For what reason do you battle sleep with uncounted all-night vigils, and destroy your body with excessive fasting? These things will not bring you a single benefit; they do not cure the envy. Every sickness of the soul, as well as the body, needs a specific medicine and has a corresponding cure."

* * *

A certain wise Father says: "He who is wronged and forgives, resembles Jesus. He, on the other hand, who does not do wrong, but nevertheless does not like to be wronged, is in the position of Adam. The unjust person, or the malicious person, or the slanderer, however, is no different from the devil."

* * *

Tradition tells us that the Apostle Iakovos, the brother of Saint John the Evangelist, at the time that he was being led to his martyrdom, met the man who had betrayed him. He stopped him and kissed him, saying: "Live in peace, brother."

Seeing such meekness, the betrayer marvelled and exclaimed with enthusiasm: "I, too, am a Christian from this day on."

After this confession, he was beheaded along with the Apostle.

* * *

"There are many monks and laymen who are believers only in words," said Saint Kallinikos of Cernika.

* * *

"If you stand by as your brother is slandered and do not support him against those who sinfully attack him, you, too, are an attacker," a spiritual Father of our day counselled a priest.

* * *

"From this day, from this hour, from this minute, let us strive to love God above all, and fulfill His holy will."

"The true Christian is a warrior fighting his way through the regiments of the unseen enemy to his heavely homeland" (Saint Herman of Alaska).

* * *

Another young man went astray, but repented so much when Divine Grace was visited upon him by the hearing of only *one* sermon, that he left the world and became a monk. He built a small hut in the desert and cried each day over his sins with great compunction. But nothing could console him.

One night Jesus appeared to him in his sleep, encircled by a heavenly light. He went near the monk with kindness: "What is wrong, young man, and why do you cry with such distress?" He asked him in His sweet voice.

"I am crying, Lord, because I fell," the sinful man said with hopelessness.

"O, then get up."

"I cannot do it alone, Lord."

So the King of Love stretched out His divine hand and helped him to get up. The monk, however, did not stop weeping.

"Why are you crying now?"

"I am in pain, my Christ, because I failed You. I wasted the riches of Your gifts on debaucheries."

The benevolent Master tenderly placed His hand on the head of the suffering sinner and cheerfully told him: "Since you suffer so much for me, I will put an end to your sorrowing for things past."

The young man looked up to thank his Savior, but He was no longer there. In the place where He had stood, a huge cross, all lighted, formed. Delivered at last from the weight of sin, he fell down and venerated it.

With gratitude in his soul, after this vision, the young man went back to the town in order to become a more fervent advocate of repentance and to guide many other strayers to Christ.

* * *

A certain very old hermit fell ill and suffered alone, for there was no one to be found in the wilderness to care for him. Seeing his patience, God enlightened a young monk to go to his hut. When he found him, gravely ill, he lovingly stayed at his side to ease him. He washed him, made him a mattress from straw, and cooked him a little food.

"Believe me, brother," the elder told the monk with gratitude, "I had completely forgotten that there were such comforts for humans."

The next day the brother took him wine to give him strength. When the elder saw it, he became tearful and murmured: "I had not expected such attention until my death."

* * *

SECTION 4

"When people honor you, humble yourself all the more at that moment, and say in your mind: 'If they truly knew who I were, they would show me no regard at all.' In this way, you will not cause injury to your soul," a wise elder said.

* * *

In the era that asceticism flowered in Egypt, there lived an orphan girl named Taisia. When her kind parents died, they left as an inheritance, first, above all other things, their piety and love for the poor and strangers; and, after that, a large home and a great deal of money to manage.

The girl, out of great reverence for the hermits, made her home a guest-house, as a service to them, and, when they came down to the city to sell their handicrafts, she looked after them with all of her heart. Over the years, however, Taisia's money was used up and she, herself, began to be in want. Thereupon, she was thrust in the midst of evil and currupt people. They exploited her misfortune and, with their cunning, led her into depravity. The beautiful Taisia became a well-known prostitute.

When the Fathers of the desert learned of the downfall of the orphan girl, they decided to do all that was in their hands to save her.

"When she had the means, she showed us every possible consideration," they said among themselves. "Now that her soul is in danger, it is *we* who must pay our debt to her." So they entrusted this delicate and difficult task to Abba John the Short.

56

At first he hesitated. The task seemed infeasible. At last, however, so as not to be disobedient to the Fathers, he decided to go down to the city and present himself at the house of the sinful woman. He requested the doorkeeper to escort him to her mistress.

"Get out of here, old monk," she angrily shouted at him. "First you eat up her fortune and then you still do not cease to pester her."

The Father was not discouraged. He continued to ask to see Taisia; "for something very beneficial to her," he said. In the face of his perseverence, the old woman gave in and went to inform her mistress.

"These monks are always fishing in the Red Sea and finding pearls," Taisia said. "Bring him up." She looked at herself in the mirror, straightened her hair and her clothes, splashed a little perfume on herself, and lay on her couch with the air of a fallen woman, to greet the hermit.

Abba John sorrowfully went to her room. He stood across from her. Standing and gazing at her with contempt for some time, he did not speak. Finally he said to her in a gentle voice: "In what way did our Christ offend you, Taisia, that you resist him so unmercifully?" He stopped. He could not continue. His sobs choked him. Burning tears ran from his sunken eyes. She felt ashamed.

Changing her unbecoming, lying position, she worriedly asked him: "Why are you crying, Father?"

"How can I not cry, my daughter, when I see Satan playing in your face?"

The girl was shocked. A shiver passsed through her entire body.

"Now that you have come, elder, it is too late. There remains nothing upright in me. I wallowed with it all in the mud," she silently murmured, perturbed.

She wanted to say something else, too, but she stopped. The elder stood with his hands crossed on his chest. He was praying so strongly within himself for the salvation of the girl, that it was as if he were asking for the heavens to quake.

"Can it be that there is even salvation for me *now*, Abba?"

she murmured doubtfully.

"O yes, there is, my daughter," the elder cried with anguish. "Repentance brings about salvation."

The miracle, which he had for so much time sought with his prayer, took place at that moment. Taisia fell, broken, at his feet and, with tears in her eyes, begged: "Take me away from here, Father. Show me the way to salvation."

"Follow me."

With no more talking, the girl got up and followed the elder. He was amazed how she showed no concern for her home. They made off for the road to the desert. But they had a long way yet to go, when evening fell on them. They stopped. Abba John cut some bushes and fashioned a makeshift bed for the girl.

"Sleep until dawn," he advised her. "We still have a long road ahead of us."

He removed himself some distance away. Having said his prayers, he lay down on the ground to rest, taking a hard rock as his pillow. He slept a little and then woke up in the middle of the night to continue praying. Then there appeared before his eyes a grandiose sight. From the spot where he had left the girl to sleep, a lighted path began, reaching up to heaven. Swift-winged angels were carrying up a soul, all white like a dove, to the throne of God. The Saint stood for a long time staring, overwhelmed by the vision. Afterwards, he started over to where Taisia was. He shouted, to wake her. She did not hear. So, he lightly moved her. She was dead.

Deeply moved, the hermit knelt at the side of the soulless body and gave himself over to fervent prayer. Then he perceived a sweet voice assuring his confused mind: "Even a short time of *profound* contrition is enough for the soul to find the way to salvation."

* * *

"Thrice-blessed is the monk who endures labors and trials, being thankful to God," Abba Kopris used to say.

Once Abba Kopris himself became gravely ill and astounded the brothers with his admirable patience. Not one time did he ask that his slightest request be fulfilled, and prayer was not for one moment absent from his lips."

* * *

A certain brother was tormented for a full nine years by an evil thought. Each day he wept and said, in reproach of himself: "I am to blame for this. I will lose my soul."
He struggled arduously. In vain, however. It was impossible to get rid of his thought. In the end, his resistance yielded. He fell into desperation. "I have now lost my soul," he thought. "Why should I stay in the desert for no reason? I will return to the world."
So it was that he set on his way for the city. But as he was walking, heavy-hearted, he heard a voice behind him: "O unfortunate man! Is this how you trample on the wreath of unfading flowers which you have been weaving, with your patience, for nine years? Go back to finish it!"
The balm of consolation flowed over the brother's heart. With a steadfast pace he now set himself on the road back to the desert. And our good God made his thought vanish.

* * *

"If two brothers quarrel," says Saint Ephraim the Syrian, "the one who first asks forgiveness will earn the crown of victory. And assent will be produced on the other's behalf, if he does not treat his brother with scorn, but is eager to make peace between them."

* * *

"You cannot cast out malice with malice," Saint Poimen says. "Thus, if your brother does you some wrong, try to repay him with good. Only goodness can conquer malice."

* * *

"My brother, be always calm and look after yourself. Do not let your soul be influenced by any person's standing, whether he is of low social status, or of great status, or even of the ruling class. No one among men can ransom you from the inextinguishable fire of hell. Notice what the Holy Spirit of God says: 'Of what benefit is it to a man, if he gains the whole world, yet suffers the loss of his soul?'

"So, do not lose the glory of God by reason of the temporary glory and honor of men, through eating, drinking, or through any other material thing whatever. All of these things perish and are destroyed. Deeds, however, every one of them, both good and evil, are recorded, and they remain everlasting.

"My brother, turn your mind toward heavenly things and reflect on *them,* and *not* on earthly goods, which are temporal, that you might attain all that the heavenly Father has promised to his children, and enjoy the glory which is enjoyed by all those who have pleased God, that is, the Saints" (Saint Ephraim).

* * *

"An irascible man, even if he is capable of raising the dead," said Abba Agathon, "will not be received into the Kingdom of Heaven."

* * *

"A complaining, vindictive monk, prone to anger, cannot exist," said Abba Poimen. "That is to say that, any who have such faults are not actually monks, even if they wear the schema."

* * *

"When I was young," Abba Isidoros relates, "I went down to the city to sell my baskets and, feeling anger seize me, I left my baskets and returned, running, to my cell."

* * *

"Contemplate God's providence continually and insatiably in the books of the divine teachers, for in this way the mind will be given guidance in perceiving the marvelous order in God's creation and in knowing His works. Thereby, the mind is strengthened and forms, through its profound study, sensations and thoughts which glitter with light; finally, the study of the books of the divine teachers helps the mind advance with spiritual purity to the deepest knowledge of God's creation.

"When you study, take care to be calm in all things, free from excessive worldly concern and from commotion, which the various events of life create in the soul. Only then will you be able to enjoy the sweet taste of the understanding of these writings. The soul will feel their deepest sense and, being carelessly impressed by them, it will rejoice mystically.

"Reverence the books and teachings of genuine writers, and do not think of them as you would of works which have only external worth and disregard divine words, so that you do not remain blind to the end of your life and live in want of their profit, so beloved by God.

"Devote yourself to the reading of divine writings, which reveal to man the way to the clearest vision of divine magnificence, even if, immediately, you do not taste the sweetness of these sensations, your mind not yet having been cleansed and not having been removed from the material.

"When you get up for meditation and your rule of prayer, instead of the worldly occupation of your mind with all that you see and hear, dwell on the deepest understanding of the sensations about which you read in the divine writings, and forget concern over worldly things; thereby, your mind will begin to be cleansed. And this is the meaning of the saying: 'The soul is aided by reading when it stands in prayer and, in turn, it is enlightened in reading by prayer.'

"Until a person receives the Comforter into his soul, he has need of the Divine Scriptures, in order to imprint on his heart the remembrance of all that is good, and, through continual reading, to renew within himself an impulse toward good. In this way, the soul will protect itself from the subtle paths of sin, it still not having acquired the power of the Holy Spirit to remove from the mind forgetfulness, which erases remembrances beneficial to the soul and compels the mind to scatter itself and roam in fruitless things.

"For when, at last, this power of the Spirit seats itself in the faculty of the soul, which operates with the aid of this Spirit, then the commandments of the Spirit, instead of the law of the Scriptures, take root in the heart, and thus the person learns mystically by the Spirit, without having need of perceptible material in his task of spiritual building" (Abba Isaak).

* * *

The youngest brothers of the skete surrounded Saint Makarios one day and asked him to teach them how to pray.

"The greatest mistake we make in praying," he replied, "is verbosity. It is sufficient for a man to learn to elevate his mind to the heavenly and to say with all of his soul, 'Lord, have mercy, as you know and as you will.' This is prayer.

"Again, when he feels the attack of the devil strongly upon him, or the rebellion of the lower passions, let him run with faith to the Heavenly Father and let him cry to Him, not with his mouth, but with his heart: 'Lord, help me.' He knows the way to help a soul which draws near to Him with trust."

* * *

"If the desire of the Heavenly Kingdom burns in your soul like a lighted torch, be sure that your soul will quickly become its heir," Abba Iperechios tells us.

* * *

A very holy man of our own days, living in a place where the Holy Orthodox Church suffers the heaviest persecution, was pursued by the God-hating agents of the state. Having taken refuge in the forest, the pious faithful regularly took him and the Fathers with him food and supplies. Having done so once on a snowy day, the Fathers noticed that their benefactors had left a telltale path in the snow, on their way out of the forest. They realized that their refuge could easily be found simply by following this path. In desperation, they turned to their holy elder, who fervently prayed to the Blessed Theotokos for aid. So acceptable was his holy prayer that, forthwith, a flock of birds descended and, pecking away at the path left by the faithful, obliterated any evidence of their visit.

* * *

It is said of a pious abbess, living in our times, that she was once returned to her convent by the authorities, after having been missing for some days. She had been found sitting in the gutters of the worst parts of the city, seemingly a derelict, suffering the abuse of passers-by. Her spiritual daughters, astonished by these circumstances, hastened to ask her for an explanation. She told them: "You, my children, have me to teach you obedience. But I have no one."

And so, voluntarily suffering the abuse of others, the holy woman struggled to maintain her humility.

* * *

"I feel myself continually sunk up to my neck in the mud of sin," Abba Paul said with humility, "and I weep, crying to Jesus with all of the strength of my heart: 'Lord, have mercy on me.' "

* * *

Abba Bissarion, those who had the fortune of knowing him say, passed his life without cares, as do the birds of the sky. Things of his own he did not have—not even the absolutely necessary; for example, a book or a second garment. The garment he wore was so old that not even the last beggar would have lowered himself to take it. He never acquired a hut, nor did he ever stay under a roof. He roamed the deserts, ravaged by the cold and the heat. If his course took him by some hermitage or monastery, he would sit at the gate and weep, as though he had been rescued from some shipwreck.

"Why are you grieving like this, brother?" those not yet familiar with him would ask.

"Because of the wealth which I lost and my previous nobility and glory," was his usual answer. It was impossible to convince him to enter, in order to offer him hospitality. The brothers would take him a little food there, outside, where he sat.

"Eat a little and have hope in God. He will give you back what you lost," they would comfort him, believing that he was really the victim of a shipwreck.

"I am not worthy to receive it," Abba Bissarion would sigh. "But as long as I live, I shall not cease seeking it." Then they would understand that he was speaking of heavenly goods.

It is further said of him that he once stood upright for forty days and nights on a pile of wood, in order to conquer sleep. He had never lain down to sleep. It was sufficient for him to sleep a little while standing or sitting on a rock.

* * *

"If God, in his forbearance, tolerates us when we serve sin," said a wise elder, "how much more will His mercy strengthen us, when we struggle for what is good."

* * *

It is said of a brother that each time his thoughts seduced him and said, "let today slip by and repent tomorrow," this wise brother would answer: "Today I shall show repentance with my deeds; as for tomorrow, let God's will be done."

* * *

The ruinous passion of rancor strips the soul of divine grace and leaves even the most virtuous person a wretched corpse. Heed what we read in the ancient martyrology of the Church: "A pious young Christian, Nikephoros, lived in a certain city of the East at the time of the Emperor Valerian. In the same city, there lived a certain Christian zealot, the Priest Saprikios. The two of them were joined closely together by an intimate spiritual friendship. Nikephoros, being young, revered and showed obedience to Saprikios. He, in turn, loved and counselled the youth. But the devil, who despises every good, sowed dissension between them and broke up their beautiful friendship. Saprikios, forgetting that he was a servant of Jesus, who is gentle and forgiving, so hated Nikephoros that he did not even wish to see him before his eyes. Many times the good youth tried to visit his old friend to ask his forgiveness. And he sent others on his behalf to seek reconciliation. But everything was a wasted effort in the face of the stubborn refusal of the priest.

Just at that time a great persecution against Christians fell upon the entire East. First among those caught in the native land of Nikephoros and Saprikios, was the Priest Saprikios, and they tortured him to make him deny his faith and sacrifice to the idols. In the beginning, he withstood his tortures bravely; he confessed his devotion to Christ boldly and was finally thrown into jail until the prefect of his city was to decide in what way he would be put to death.

Nikephoros agonizingly followed the sufferings of his friend and, when he was placed in jail, the youth paid the jailkeeper a great deal of money to let him see his friend. When he went near him, he fell at his feet and, with fervent tears, asked him to make friends again so as not to separate forever with enmity between them.

"Forgive me," he told the priest, "I am to blame for everything."

But Saprikios remained as cold as marble and unmoved like a rock by the entreaties of his friend, not condescending even to cast a glance towards him. Nikephoros left, broken by the incomprehensible behavior of the priest.

Finally, it was decided that Saprikios would be beheaded by the sword. The executioners led him to the place of execution and Nikephoros followed behind, begging reconciliation. He shuddered at the thought that shortly his friend would pass into eternity, while a chasm of hate that could not be bridged separated them. Saprikios continued to remain as hard as granite.

When the great moment arrived, that the confessor was at last to receive the wreath of victory and his name was to be inscribed among the names of the glorious martyrs, divine grace left him. Just as the executioner raised his sword to cut off his head, Saprikios was taken aback, as though waking from a deep stupor. Frightened, he asked why they had him tied.

"You are condemned to death, because you refused to sacrifice to the gods of the state," answered the surprised executioner, who for the first time had chanced to have a Christian who lost courage under his sword.

"I will make sacrifices," the denier dared to utter.

Nikephoros, who had followed this whole unbelievable scene, which had unfolded so quickly before him, and who had seen a divine angel waiting to crown the martyr, stepped out and shouted to the executioner: "Jesus wants a martyr with him on this day. I am a Christian. Behead *me*."

Nikephoros took the place of Saprikios in martyrdom, while to Saprikios' rancor was added the stigma of denial.

* * *

A young Abbot was counselled thus, in our own day, by a holy man: "Today many people, wishing for an excuse not to do what God asks of them, find fault with the teaching of the Holy Church and reject correct Christian belief. Instead, they choose to believe what they wish. This is akin to a man not wishing to believe that he will die, simply because the notion does not comfort him. Not only will he fail to prepare for death, as one ought to do, but he will inevitably find himself in the snare of death. Correct belief is not based on what we wish were true, but on Truth itself."

* * *

Said a wise man in our times: "Most people fear the loss of a loved one because, not attending to their own salvation, they have time to waste thinking about the salvation of others.''

* * *

Advises another contemporary monk: "In these days, monks are so hated that laymen, even wishing to love them, cause them harm. Seeing in monks what they cannot realize in themselves, they wish to erase any trace of the holy life. This can be done even by those with supposedly good intentions, who, however, do not know their inner, evil goals.''

* * *

A pious Orthodox scholar of modern times constantly stressed that worldly knowledge is of no consequence to the spiritual man. But equally strongly he resisted ignorance and those who teach that man need not use his intellect. "The intellect," he said, "must serve the spiritual. The *correct* and humble use of our minds in spiritual pursuits is commended by the Fathers.''

He often related that some of the desert Fathers had come to believe that God, man having been created in His image, was like a human being: "Even Abba Serapion, an old and deeply pious ascetic, we read in the 'Conferences' of Saint John Cassian, believed in an anthropomorphic vision of God. Only when a learned monk from Cappadocia convinced him that both Scripture and the Orthodox Church support the view that God is 'unmeasurable' and 'incomprehensible,' and 'cannot be limited by a human frame or likeness,' did Serapion repent of his misbelief.

"When the great desert holy man, Abba Isaak, was asked how such a pious ascetic as Serapion could have been seduced by demons to believe wrongly, he answered: 'This error is not, as you think, a modern delusion from the demons, but an inheritance from the ignorance of the ancient heathens.' We learn here that piety and simplicity do not excuse ignorance or prevent its erroneous consequences. We must all begin our spiritual lives knowing properly with our intellects what the Church teaches of God. Otherwise, we might all cry with the repentant Serapion: 'Woe is me! They have taken my God from me and I have none to grasp.' If we know of God first with our minds and *then* with our hearts, He can never be taken away. Knowledge and humility, not ignorance, are our goals.''

* * *

ἸΗϹΟΫ̀

ΚΎΡΙΕ

ΧΡΙϹΤΈ

ἘΛΈΗϹΟΝ ΜΕ

SECTION 5

"A certain youth," Abba John of Likopoulos relates to us, "swept away by the pleasures of the world, had sunk into the mud of dissoluteness. It happened, however, that he came to his senses, like the prodigal son, and sought the way of return to his Father's house. He left the world, to find redemption in the desert. His refuge was an abandoned tomb. Closed away in this unusual prison, his injured soul wept bitterly.

"The angels rejoiced at this; but the spirits of evil, who saw their prey so unexpectedly slip from their hands, lost no time in making an assault. They would gather around the tomb at night and say with rage: 'Where are you athlete (struggler)? Why have you forsaken us, after such friendship? After tasting everything to excess, you now decide to become holy. It is too late to pretend to be reformed now, hoping for mercy.'

" 'Come on out, you ignorant man,' other spirits would shout. 'Your companions are waiting for you.'

" 'You unfortunate man,' the most cunning spirits would whisper, 'there is no salvation for you. You will quicky find death and eternal damnation there where you are hiding.'

"With what malice they endeavored to bring him to despair. But the brave struggler was too determined to die better, never to return to his former ways. He asked for divine aid with fervent entreaties, scorning the demonic fantasies. Then one night the devil became more frightening.

" 'If you do not come out immediately, you will never escape from my hands.' And since he did not, of course, listen to the devil, the devil set upon him and left him nearly dead from his

69

blows. He took vengeance in this way.

"The monk's relatives, meanwhile, uneasy with his sudden disappearance, were looking everywhere for him. Finally they found him in terrible shape in the tomb. But as much as they insisted, they remained unable to persuade him to follow them.

"Yet another night, the demons set upon him with unrestrained rage and would have killed him with their fierce beatings; but they did not have the power. The athlete did not waver. He preferred to lose this ephemeral life, rather than to defile his body and soul again with the germ of sin, after having repented. So the demons recognized their defeat.

" 'You conquered us, you conquered us,' they shouted, lamenting, and disappeared, never even daring to tempt him further.

"Being freed, thereby, from every trial, the formerly dissolute monk remained in the tomb until the end of his life, and was made worthy to perform miracles, in order to show the power of repentance."

* * *

A virgin, devoted to God, told the following story to her spiritual Father, and he wrote it down exactly as he heard it from her mouth, so that others might learn of it and benefit spiritually.

"My parents, who brought me into the world, were completely different in character and took opposite directions in life.

"My father was a very kind man, gentle, humble, lenient, unimaginably compassionate, prudent, and sober. His health was frail. As long as I can remember, most of the time I saw him sick in bed, pale and weak. He suffered, however, with admirable patience. Never did anyone hear him complain about his distressing illness.

"In the short intervals during which he was well, he watched over his lands. The greater part of his profits he divided among the poor. With the remainder, he looked after his small family, that is, himself, my mother, and me. In addition to his other virtues, my kind father had also attained that of silence. He rarely spoke (many thought him dumb); and this, because he prayed continually to God with his mind and with his heart.

"My mother, on the contrary, was a typical woman of the world. She passionately loved a good time, diversions, many ornaments, and clothing. She led such an extravagant life, that we always had economic worries. She fought and quarreled continuously at home and away from home. And so talkative and nosey was the poor woman, that she knew well all of the news in our small city and even anything that took place outside of it. She was so egotistical that she took care of herself first and her family afterwards. She showed not the slightest love for her husband and, with her obvious disaffection, his torments were thus ever greater. Yet, despite all of her faults and the incontinent life which she led, she had her health and a strong body. I do not remember her ever to have been ill.

"While I was still a young girl, my father died after an agonizing illness. And something happened at his death that, indeed, left a lasting impression on me: There was such unprecedented bad weather, winds, rain, thunder and lightning, that it was impossible to get out to bury him. So, we kept the body unburied in our house for three days. Finally, two men from among our relatives were compelled, with great difficulty, to take the body to the cemetery and bury it in any way possible, since we could no longer endure seeing the corpse in the house. Since he did not even have a funeral, my father was scorned even at his death. Indeed, some evil neighbors, seeing such great misfortunes, spoke against him: 'Who knows what sins he committed, since God will not even allow him to be buried?'

"My mother, less hindered after the death of my father, succumbed to moral decline and made our house a place of debauchery. But she did not live long. She died suddenly, having in the meantime wasted all that remained of my father's estate. Her friends, however, gave her a magnificent funeral. And the weather was wonderful. This I especially noticed.

"Having passed the age of childhood, and the uneasiness of young womanhood having begun to take control of me, I found myself all alone in the world and in great perplexity as to what direction I should take. My thoughts tormented me.

" 'I must, without fail, make it on my own in life, since I no longer have any guardians,' I said to myself. 'But what way shall I choose? I have before me different examples: that of my mother and that of my father. He was good, but unhappy. Persecuted in life and in death.' It was impossible for me to get his unburied body out of my mind. 'If he was pleasing God, why did God torment him so?' My mother had not led a moral life. I well understood that. However, she had as many goods as anyone could desire, wealth, comfort, and many friends, and she left the world happy, one might say.

"The more I thought about the matter and made comparisons in my young mind, the more I turned away from misfortune to follow my mother's life. God, in his benevolence, however, showed mercy and guided me to the straight path in the following, unusual manner: "One night I fell into bed, occupied once more with the same thoughts. I had a revealing vision. I felt the door of my room open, and a young man with a luminous face and of unimaginable majesty entered. He came close to me. As though searching the most hidden things of my heart, he cast a piercing glance at me.

" 'What are you thinking about?' he asked me in an unusually austere, but melodious voice.

"I was surprised and became frightened. I tried hard to speak. He intervened: 'Your thoughts were immediately revealed to me.'

"The more austere this unknown interrogator became, the more I was paralyzed by fear. Since he had received no reply, he revealed on his own the thoughts which were so tormenting me. He told me in detail every thought which had passed through my mind, and which only I knew, so that I could neither deny the thoughts nor offer excuses for them. So, I fell at his feet, as though condemned, and asked him, sobbing, to forgive me. He seemed to feel sorry for me, because he immediately changed his mien.

" 'Follow me,' he commanded.

"He took me by the hand and, like lightning, transported me to a boundless plain, filled with light and beauty. I will not attempt to describe it, for the indescribable is not describable.

Happy beings were serenely enjoying this supernatural beauty. Among them, I recognized my father. And he saw me. He came to me and took me in his arms. I felt such assurance and happiness there. I did not want to be separated from him ever again. I clasped onto him and asked him never to let me go.

" 'Keep me near you forever, kind father.'

" 'What you ask for cannot be at this time.' His voice became more serious.

" 'If you follow my steps, you will prepare a place for yourself here. It depends on what you desire.' He looked at me with tenderness and gathered up my hair to wipe away my tears. My escort nodded to me to follow him again. But I did not want to leave my father's arms. So, he came and pulled me by the hand.

" 'You also need to see your mother,' he said.

"I followed him, sorrowful that he had separated me from my happiness. Now we descended. We went deeper and deeper to an unclean, dark, and dreary place. I lost my breath from the stench and my fear. Monstrous figures were roaming all about. Unfortunate souls were being tormented without mercy by an inextinguishable flame. In their midst, I saw my mother, buried up to her neck in what appeared to me like foul-smelling lava. Her cries came forth heart-rendingly, her groans were uninterrupted, and the fearful gnashing of her teeth tore my heart apart. She must have known me, because she broke out in uncontrolled lamentation.

" 'Woe is me, wretch that I am. Look what such little pleasure earned me: despair and torment without end.'

"Desperate words! I was nearly mortified by my grief. My unfortunate mother turned and looked at me.

" 'Have pity, my child, on the one who gave birth to you and raised you,' she began to cry desperately. She stretched out her hand, so that I could take her out of that grief.

"What could I do? My soul was torn by sadness. I stretched out my hand, thinking that I could help her, who brought me into the world. I felt such pain at approaching the lava, that I broke into loud cries. I stirred up the neighborhood. Shortly, my house was full of people. They found me in a bad condition.

Many thought I had lost my senses. It was impossible to explain what had happened to me. I showed them the frightful wound that was left on my hand by the fire, so that they would understand that I was sufffering because of it. I remained in bed a long time, gravely ill. When, by the grace of God, I became well, without delay I followed my father's path; and I hope that, in His mercy, my Lord will save me and make me worthy to share in his happiness.''

* * *

An elderly Abba went down to the city one day to sell his baskets. Exhausted by the journey, he went and sat on the steps of a large house that he came across on his way.

At that moment, the rich landlord of the house was in the throes of death. While the Abba was resting, having no idea what was happening inside, he suddenly saw a great number of black horsemen, vicious in appearance, galloping towards him. They got off of the pitch-black horses at the outside door and rushed into the house.

The elder understood, and followed them up to the room of the dying man. When the dying man saw the horsemen, he uttered heart-rending cries: "My God, save me." The horsemen ridiculed him harshly.

"Can it be that you *now* remember God, in the evening of your life? It is too late to think of Him. Why did you not call on Him during the daylight hours of your life? Now you belong to us."

As soon as the men had said these things, they violently tore away his soul and went away with triumphant shouts of joy.

The Abba was left dumb, as though dead, by his sorrow and fright. When, after a great deal of time, he came to his senses, he related all that God had revealed to him, for the benefit of others.

* * *

"Reflect each day on those things in which you have erred. And if you call on God with contrition concerning these faults, He will surely forgive you of them. Question yourself always, as long as you live, to discover where you fall short; surely at the time of your death, then, you will not suffer from the horrible agony of fear because of your faults. Be always ready to encounter God, and thereby you will be ready to carry out His will. Every single day examine carefully whichever of your passions you have been able to conquer—never trusting in yourself, supposing that somehow with your own power you accomplished something; for God is merciful and *He* gave you the power to be victorious.

"When, each day, you rise from your bed, remember that you will give an accounting to God for your every deed, for your every word, as well as for your every thought. Thus, you will not sin before God; rather, fear of Him will dwell with you" (Abba Isaias).

* * *

"My brothers, we are spiritual merchants. Indeed, we resemble the merchants of this present life, who each day take account of their profits and losses; and, when this accounting confirms that they have suffered a loss, they reflect and see how they can rectify the loss.

"You, too, my beloved, must act this way; every day, morning and evening, you must take precise account of your business activities. In the evening, as a nightly self-inspection and collection of your thoughts, reflect and converse sincerely with yourself, saying: 'Was I perhaps lax in some instance, annoying God? Did I perhaps fall into idle talk? Did I perhaps fail to show concern for the spiritual welfare of my brother, or irritate him? Did I maybe speak ill of someone? I wonder if, when my lips were singing hymns to God, perhaps my mind was thinking of worldly vanities. Perhaps carnal desires troubled me and I gladly accepted this trouble. Perhaps I was absorbed by bodily concerns and I completely abandoned the memory of God.'

"Think about these and similar things, in the nightly collecting of your thoughts, and if you discover that at some point you have suffered a loss, take care to rectify that loss. Groan and cry, persistently asking God to help you, so that you will never again suffer losses in the same things.

"And when morning comes, when taking account, think about the following and say: 'I wonder how I passed this night. Did I gain something from it, or did I incur a loss? Did my mind also slumber, along with my body? Did I have spiritual tears? Perhaps I fell asleep while kneeling. Did I perhaps accept the attack of evil thoughts and not hasten to repulse them, but receive them in a voluptuous way?'

"Examining yourself carefully in this way, if you then note that you have been overcome somewhere, struggle to make amends for your defeat and to establish a guard in your heart, so as not to become a victim of the same thing again.

"If you always take care thus, you will preserve your spiritual merchandise, making it secure in the treasury of heaven" (Saint Ephraim).

* * *

A young man, led astray by the fearful power of bad habits, often fell into deep sin. He did not quit struggling, however. After each fall, he shed burning tears and prayed to God with these painful words: "Lord, save me, whether I desire it or not. I, like the dust that I am, am easily dragged down by the mud of sin. You, however, have the power to stop me. It is not wondrous, my God, if You have mercy on the righteous, or if You save the virtuous, for they are worthy to taste of Your goodness. Show Your mercy and benevolence to me, a sinner, Lord, and save me in a wondrous way; for, in all my wretchedness, I, unfortunate man that I am, flee only to You."

The youth said these things with contrition, both when he was taken over by passion and when he was calm. A certain time, when he was once more conquered, after an agonizing resistance, he kneeled and repeated the same words, shedding a river of tears. His invincible hope in divine mercy irritated the devil. He appeared before the youth in a total rage and shouted:

"Wretch! Do you not feel a little ashamed when you dare to pray and bring God's name to your lips, in such a state as yours? You should learn once and for all that there is no salvation for you,"

The brave struggler was not afraid, nor did he abandon his hope, as the devil expected.

"And you should know that this room is like a forge," the young man boldly answered him. "You make a strike with the hammer and then you receive one. I will not cease battling you with repentance and with prayer, until that time that you are weary of battling me with sin."

"Let it so be, then," the devil shouted with malice. "From now on I am no longer battling you, so as not to increase the spoils of your patience." Then he became invisible.

From that moment, the youth's struggle ceased. However, not for a moment did he cease watching over himself, crying frequently when he would recall his sins.

"Bravo! You have won," the enemy sometimes whispered in his mind, in order, now, to pull the youth down into pride.

"I curse this accomplishment," the youth would answer scornfully. "Do you really suppose that God wants a person to lose the purity of his soul by foul deeds and, afterwards, to sit and weep?"

* * *

A certain youth, who was preparing to follow the monastic life, went to consult Abba Photios regarding how to behave in the brotherhood. The wise elder, besides other things, also told him these profitable things: "Avoid as much as possible, my child, creating for yourself a reputation as an agitator. Never say: 'I am not eating at the common table of the brothers at the meal after Liturgy on Sunday,' or 'I am not going to the gatherings (monastery councils).' Try not to separate yourself from the others in anything, and see that you imitate the most pious brothers. In this way, you will avoid any human praise and you will attain humility."

* * *

Patriarch Theophilos and the prefect of Alexandria once went to Abba Arsenios' hut to talk with him. They asked him to give them some word of advice.

"If I do, do you promise to follow it?" the great hesychast asked.

"Yes, you have our word," they answered him.

"Ah, listen well, then. Wherever you hear that the sinner Arsenios is to be found, go far away from there and do not attempt to converse with him."

The visiting officials were not only not dissatisfied, but they showed wonderment at the great humility of the elder.

* * *

A pious, young man went to visit a certain desert elder.

"How are you getting along, Abba," he asked.

"Very badly, my child."

"Why, Abba?"

"I have been here forty years," the elder answered, sighing deeply, "doing nothing other than cursing my own self each day, inasmuch as in the prayers I offer, I say to God, 'Accursed are those who deviate from Your commandments.' "

Hearing the hermit speak in this way, the young man marveled at his humility and decided to emulate him.

* * *

Abba Matoes said: "Three elders went to Abba Paphnoutios, who was called the 'Great Head,' so that he might tell them something. And the elder said, 'What do you want me to tell you about, something pertaining to the body or something spiritual?'

" 'Something spiritual,' they said.

"And the elder told them: 'Go, loving affliction more than comfort, dishonor more than glory, and giving more than receiving.' "

* * *

Abba Daniel tells us that Abba Arsenios related the following, supposedly about someone else, but actually in reference to himself:

"While a certain elder was sitting in his cell, he heard a voice say to him, 'Come, so that I can show you what people do.' So he got up and went immediately out of his cell. The voice then led him to a place where he was shown an Ethiopian, who was cutting wood and placing it in a big pile. He tried to pick up the pile, but he could not. And instead of taking away from the pile, he just cut more wood and added to it. And this continued for a long time. Then, proceeding farther on, he was shown a man who was standing beside a well, drawing water. But he was emptying it into a cistern full of holes, and thus the water was running back into the well. Then he was further told: 'Come, and I will show you something else.' He saw a church and two horsemen, who were carrying a piece of wood, one at each end of it. They wanted to enter through the portals of the church, but they could not, since they were holding the board sideways. One would not humble himself to the other, so as to let him go in first, and thereby to put the board in the right position to enter. Therefore, they remained outside the church.

"The voice said: 'These men are those who take a proud stand, thinking they should act in such a manner, without becoming humble in order to correct themselves and walk the lowly path of Christ. Thus, they remain outside the Kingdom of God.'

" 'As for the man cutting wood, he is like a very sinful man. Instead of repenting, he adds sins to his sins. Finally, the man who was taking water from the well is like a person who does good deeds, yet, since he defiles them with bad intentions, wastes both his good deeds and his gain.'

"So, every person must be vigilant in all that he does, so that his efforts are not in vain."

* * *

John, the disciple of Abba Paul, was a paradigm of obedience. The Fathers relate the following event regarding him:

"A short distance away from their hut was a cave, inside which a hyena had made its lair. One day the elder saw some wild onions growing thereabouts and he sent John to pick some, so he could cook them.

" 'What do I do if the hyena chances to come out?' the young man asked.

" 'Tie it up and bring it here,' the elder jokingly said.

"The good disciple went to fulfill his elder's command. But just as he had anticipated, the fearful beast fell upon him. The young monk, however, not only did not hesitate, but rushed to tie it up. Then the following unusual thing took place. Instead of the disciple being afraid, the beast was afraid and ran into the desert to save itself. John chased behind it and shouted:

" 'Stop, now! The Abba told me to tie you up.'

"After much effort, he caught the hyena, tied it up, and took it to his elder. In the meantime, the Abba, seeing how late it was, became uneasy and had already gone out to meet him. Thus he saw the disciple coming, bearing the bound beast behind him, and marvelled at the power of obedience.

"To John, however, he did not show any surprise. Indeed, on the contrary, to make him humble, he shouted, with feigned austerity:

" 'You silly man, why did you bring this mad dog here?'

"Therewith, he untied the wild beast and let it go free, to return to its lair."

* * *

"The carefree monk, who has tasted the sweetness of having no personal possessions," a certain Father says, "feels that even the *rason* (cassock) which he wears and the jug of water in his cell are a useless burden, because these things, too, sometimes distract his mind."

* * *

It is said of a certain elder that he showed special affection for those who despised him and in any way dishonored him.

"These are our friends," he used to say, "because they lead us to humility. Those who honor and praise us do injury to our souls. The Scriptures also say: 'those who regard you well seduce you.' "

* * *

"When you get up from your bed, brother," a certain elder advises, "say to yourself: 'body, work in order to support yourself. Soul, be sober in order to save yourself.' "

* * *

A certain monk in our times was slandered by someone considered by others to be very holy. The slandered monk was perplexed and fell into such despair that even his body began to suffer. He asked himself, "How is it that someone thought to be holy and respected by so many would have such little understanding and hurt another person, under the guise of protecting the faith? After all, I am being attacked for supposed personal immorality, not heresy." This torment dwelled in the monk's mind.

Finally a very wise man of spiritual discretion told him: "If your attacker were really holy, he would probably not cause you this great spiritual and physical harm. But if you dare to judge him and to say, 'by this, I *know* that he is not holy,' then the spiritual harm to you will be even greater. Leave the final judgment to God, avoid the man, and pray in your soul that God will show him what he has done to you, whether out of ignorance or ill will, so that he might repent. Above all, pray for him with fervor. In this way God will grant you peace of soul, which surpasses bodily health."

In this way the monk suffered his torments, not in vain, but to his spiritual profit, dying shortly after with a peaceful heart.

* * *

"Woe to him who is honored beyond his worth," a certain

Father says. "The damage his soul suffers is irreparable. Fortunate is the man who is scorned by men, for glory awaits him in heaven."

* * *

"Woe to the man whose reputation exceeds his deeds," said a certain elder.

And again on another occasion: "Do not avoid being scorned, brother."

* * *

"What is humility, Abba?" the brothers of the skete asked a certain elder.

"Humility, my children," he answered, "is to forgive another immediately if he offends you, without waiting for him to ask your forgiveness."

"You can find no shorter road to heaven than humility," another Father said.

"Anyone who praises a man to his face," a certain elder said, "delivers him up for the devil to do battle against him."

* * *

"Anyone who shows charity to his brother," a certain Father says, "had best do so as though he were showing charity to himself. Such acts of charity bring a man near to God."

* * *

"There are people," one elder said, "who, while willing to give alms to the poor, are made by the devil to count their donations down to the last penny, so that he might deprive them of the reward for beneficence.

"I once chanced to visit a friend of mine, a priest, on the day that he was distributing alms to the poor of his parish. Just by coincidence, a poor widow came and asked to be given a little wheat.

" 'Fetch your sack, so I can put some in,' the priest told her. The woman got it.

" 'It is awfully big, my dear,' my friend somewhat brusquely told her. She became all red from her embarrassment, perhaps because there was a stranger present when she was reprimanded.

"When she left, I told my friend: 'You do not mean to tell me that you are selling the wheat to the woman, do you Father?'

" 'Well, since it was charity,' I told him, 'what need was there to scrutinize the amount and to shame the poor woman? Besides, do not forget the words of the blessed Paul: God, indeed, loves a cheerful donor.' "

* * *

At the time that Abba Lot was still young and inexperienced in the ascetic life, Abba Joseph, his elder, frequently gave him this advice: "You will never become a good monk," he told him, "unless you preserve the flame of faith unextinguished within your heart. It will enlighten you to disdain honors and comforts. Give up your own desires and, in general, keep all of the divine commandments."

* * *

"When you show charity to your poor brother," Abba Isaias advises, "do not call on him to help in your work, in order not to lose the reward for your benefaction."

* * *

A group of monks living in our own days were condemned by other monks for having many modern conveniences and comforts, which their abbot allowed them to use with discretion.

The monks who made the condemnation were so violent in their objections to the mode of life of the more comfortable monks, that a third group of monks intervened to chastise the objectors. One wise monk among them said: "Several of the monks whom you so violently condemn gave up more personal wealth, when they became monastics, than your entire family has probably known in the last few generations combined. We read in the desert Fathers of a monk who was scandalized by another monk, of high attainment, who, none the less, lived in some comfort. The former was brought to his senses when he realized that the latter monk had once had great wealth and rank. His life after becoming a monk represented the loss of many possessions and dignities. The monk who had been scandalized by this former rich man, however, had been born into poverty and had actually gained possessions in becoming a monk. This story applies quite aptly to the monks whom you are condemning.''

The condemning monks slowly learned to restrain their judgments of others.

* * *

A young monk in modern times once took an indigent and abused old nun into his monastery, since she had no place to go. He was immediately condemned by another monk who said: "The holy canons forbid you to keep a woman in a monastery for men. You have no respect for the church Fathers and, despite your intentions, you will lead your brotherhood into sin."

The young monk answered: "Even if I were to fall into the sin of fornication with this old and forgotten nun, I could repent and be forgiven. But what real forgiveness is there for a person who judges others and pretends to know that even their intentions have no meaning before God? However, if you really care for my soul, since you do not live in a brotherhood, would you assume the responsibility of caring for this old nun? I will gladly relinquish it."

The condemning monk did not reply.

* * *

Again in present times, a young woman outside the Church

came to love Holy Orthodoxy with her mind and with her heart. A very holy man told her, when she asked to be received into the Church, that she would "become Orthodox drop by drop."

Confronted by great difficulties in accepting Orthodoxy while living in a society which did not value the stern and sometimes foreign ways of the faith, the young woman diverted her attention to other things. Deeply shaken by this, the priest who had tried to guide her to Orthodoxy was perplexed as to what to do. He did not wish to show his own spiritual concern, for fear of hurting his own soul. Yet he did not wish to suffer the loss of this young woman's soul. He therefore sought the advice of a spiritual man, who told him: "If a truly holy man said that she would become Orthodox drop by drop, then this means that her Orthodoxy will come to her like the rain from heaven—by God's own will, in His time, and by His mercy. Keep silent and pray for her."

* * *

Another monk in modern times advises: "Do not let those who shout about bringing sinners to God detract you from first saving yourself. If you lose yourself trying to save others, you have taken away an example that might ultimately save hundreds. This is what the Fathers teach us. We must follow this wisdom, rather than the foolish wisdom of those who would define for us a goal and a mission which God did not give us."

* * *

In writing to a young man, a holy bishop living in our times defines the ultimate spiritual crisis in this way: "Within you there arises the enormous question: 'Christ or the world?' "

* * *

SECTION 6

In an age when political considerations and supposed historical determinants mark so much the study of the history of God's people, we people of the modern times seldom understand the dedication of the Orthodox forefathers, whether Greek, Russian, Serbian, Romanian, Bulgarian, or whatever, to the great Orthodox monarchies. We are told that this dedication was nationalistic only, anchored in unworthy social and political mores having their roots in the corrupt Byzantine system. But a great Russian Father captures, in his pious words, an image of Byzantium, of Holy Russia, and of all the Orthodox realms that we seldom see today. His words should create in our hearts a nostalgia for what modern scholarship, in its spiritual poverty, has so often denied us—a nostalgia for the noble idea of a society based on the vision of God:

"Our native land is dear to us in its political entirety, in its immense geographical space and in the strength of its State institutions. But this is only a shell for its spiritual content, its inner treasure, which is called Holy Rus. If a master puts aside the precious wine, then he will also take care to preserve the vessel without which it would spill on the floor. If a good Christian loves God and is zealous in prayer, he protects and adorns the Church in which the gifts of grace are granted to him. But the vessel is precious only because in it is stored the finest liquid; in the same way the Church is holy because in it we learn to know God.

"Thus we love Russia because she preserves within herself the Russian idea, the Russian spiritual character, the Russian way of life. This idea is God's Kingdom, this character is the striving for holiness, this way of life expresses in itself the efforts of the 700-year life of the country and the 900-year life of the people to establish in the land the godliness of the Gospels, to reject everything so as to find Christ and to apply His will and the canons of the Church as the law of social life.

"Various and innumerable are those everyday spiritual oc-curences in which this historical idea of Russia is expressed. Few manage to note and define them, but this striving for inner, spiritual truth in personal and social life, this alienation from Western pride and self-love (which are the main factors of life in the West), this indifference to material prosperity—all of these features of our Russian life and our Russian soul, even though distorted by individual downfalls, constitute a special attitude of mind which is expressed in distressing dissatisfaction with westernized principles of life and in a tender, though vaguely realized, filial love for everything of one's own and for the Motherland.

"Even such inveterate westernizers as Nekrasov, Hertzen, and Turgenev experience this love, despite themselves, and if they and contemporaries like them rebuke Russia, then they on-ly skim over the surface of their souls like teenagers talking scandal to their parents, but ready to die of grief when their parents are exposed to dangers or terrible sufferings. So in both cases, there comes to light a hidden, natural deep feeling which is difficult to get rid of by idle calumny.

"Our Motherland is embodied in the character of the people, in the Gospel way of life of the people; it embodies the Kingdom of God. Our Rus is not only a legal entity or a state—no, she is a universal, all-embracing idea.

"To love her, to understand her, to take her into our soul and into the sphere of life which is dependent on each of us—therein lies our duty, therein lies our true joy, therein lies the reconcilia-tion of everything with life in general and with our lot, therein lies the need for our general prayer to rise on high."

Thus spoke Metropolitan Antony (Khrapovitsky) in 1904, before the demise of Holy Russia.

It once passed through the mind of Antonios the Great to wonder what measure of holiness he had attained. God, however, Who wished to humble his mind, showed him in a dream one night that a certain cobbler, who had a shop on one of the out-of-the-way streets of Alexandria, was better than he.

As soon as day broke, the Saint took his staff and set out for the city. He wanted to meet this renown cobbler himself and to see his virtues. With great difficulty, he found his shop, went inside, sat down beside him on his bench, and began to ask about his life.

The simple man, who could not figure out who this old monk who came so suddenly to interrogate him was, answered him ever so slowly and calmly, without taking his eyes from the shoe that he was mending.

"I do not know, Abba, if I have ever done any good. Every morning I get up and do my prayers and then I begin my work. However, I first say to myself that all the people in this city, from the very least to the very greatest, will be saved, and only I will be condemned for my many sins. And in the evening when I lie down, again I think about the same thing."

The Saint stood up in wonderment, embraced the cobbler, kissed him, and said to him with emotion: "You, my brother, like a good merchant, have easily gained the precious pearl. I have grown old in the desert, toiling and sweating, but I have not attained to your humility."

* * *

"A blossom is the beginning of fruit bearing," Saint Ephraim writes, "and submission the beginning of humility. The humble man is, as a rule, obedient, respects the lowly and the great, and shows leniency and kindness."

* * *

Abba Poimen said: "A man may seem silent, but if in his heart he condemns others, he is talking ceaselessly. Yet there may be someone else who talks from morning until night, who, because he says nothing unprofitable, is truly silent.''

* * *

"The monk should wear a garment of the kind that, if he threw it away outside his cell, no one would steal it for three days" (Abba Pambo).

* * *

"The saints are like various trees, each bearing different fruit, but watered from the same source. The practices of one saint differ from those of another, but the same Spirit works in them," said one great Father.

* * *

A certain brother asked one of the great Fathers what humility is.

"Humility, my child, is always to feel yourself sinful and worse than all other people," the elder explained. "This is a great and difficult feat. But you can accomplish it by applying yourself with unceasing labor."

"But how is it possible to see yourself as worse than all others continuously?" the brother wondered.

"Learn to see the good qualities of others and to see your own faults, asking each day for forgiveness from God for them, and you will accomplish it," the Saint advised.

* * *

"There are people," Antonios the Great said, "who, having used up all of their bodily powers in excessive asceticism, do not succeed in drawing near to God, since they lack discretion."

* * *

The Fathers call discretion the greatest of all virtues.

* * *

"A festival for the spiritual man," Saint Ephraim the Syrian writes, "is the observance of the divine commandments, and his consolation abstinence from evil. His pride is the fear of God, his real joy the day when the Heavenly King calls him to inherit His eternal riches."

* * *

"The eyes of the pig," says one Father, "are so situated that they look only at the ground. The man who has been seized by the desire for foods suffers from the same thing; he looks down all the time and is not capable of anything lofty."

* * *

"Why do the demons tremble before you, Abba?" a young monk asked Saint Isidore the Pelusian.

"Because, since the time I became a monk, I have not let any enjoyable thing enter my throat."

* * *

A wise elder gives the following advice to monks and youth alike: "Avoid eating foods which are to your liking, but, preferably, eat the simplest foods, and be thankful to God, Who also sends you these."

* * *

It is said of Abba Agathon that he lived for three years with a stone in his mouth, until he learned silence.

* * *

"Unless a man keeps the commandments of God, he cannot progress, even in a single virtue" (Abba Agathon).

* * *

As Abba Agathon and his disciple were returning to their cell one day, the young man found a green bean on the road.

"May I take it, Abba?" he asked the elder.

"Did you perhaps put it there yourself?"

"No, Abba."

"Ah, then how is it that you think you can take it?"

* * *

The devil frequently went to the cave of a certain hermit, in order to terrorize him and make him leave there. The monk not only did not lose courage, but he treated the evil spirit scornfully. So the devil, to lead him astray, appeared to him in the form of Christ.

"I am Christ," he said to him. The hermit closed his eyes.

"Why are you closing your eyes?" the devil shouted to him with irritation. "I told you that I am Christ."

"I do not wish to see Christ in this world," the hermit answered, keeping his eyes shut. With the bold reply of this man of God, the devil disappeared and never again dared to tempt him.

* * *

An elder prescribes the following rule of conduct for the monastic table: "When you sit to eat, brother, do not be overcome by the demon of gluttony, which compels you to eat in a disorderly way and in haste and to desire to taste many kinds of food together. Learn to eat modestly and in an orderly way and maintain a measure of restraint."

* * *

Saint Ephraim the Syrian, the renown teacher of asceticism, once decided to leave, for a time, his beloved silence in the desert and go down to the city. He desired to venerate the holy relics which were then found in Edessa, as well as to meet with men of the church, so as to discuss doctrinal truths with them.

He lived in an age when the correct faith was assailed on all sides by fearful heresies.

"Lord," he prayed before setting out, "Put before me a person to instruct me, when I pass through the city gate."

But at the moment that he reached the populous city of Edessa, the first person that he encountered on his way was a woman of the street, who stood and stared at him shamelessly. The Saint complained to the Lord that He had deigned to let him find the opposite of what he had asked for. Afterwards, he turned to the woman and, to evoke some shame in her, told her brusquely: "I am amazed that you do not turn red with embarrassment for daring to stare at me so persistently."

She promptly told him: "I am doing that which suits me. Being created from your rib, I should look at you. As for you, however, who were created from dust, you would do well to have your gaze constantly fixed on it."

Receiving such an exact response, the Saint thanked God with gratitude. A more beneficial lesson than this he surely could not have wanted.

* * *

A young monk, who had only shortly before left the world, was overcome by the desire to see his parents. He asked his elder for permission to go for a few days to his home. He, seeing the weakness of his disciple, sighed deeply and told him: "I am going to let you go, my child, but keep well in mind what I am going to tell you: When you set off from your home for here, you had God with you as a fellow traveler. Leaving here for your home, you will be completely alone."

* * *

Abba Longinos was once asked which virtue he considered most important of all.

"Just as pride is the greatest of all evils, since it succeeded in casting the angels from heaven to the abyss, so humility is the greatest of all virtues. It had the power to raise the sinner from the abyss up to heaven. For this reason, the Lord blesses, before all others, the poor in spirit."

* * *

"I prefer collapse with humility to victory with pride," says another Father.

* * *

And Abba Sarmatias said: "I prefer a sinful person, who knows his faults and is humbled, over a self-complacent person of virtue."

* * *

"Humility, with no extended labors, has saved many," another elder says. "This is verified by the tax collector and the prodigal son, who were received by God because of the few humble words that they said."

* * *

A monk of a large monastery, negligent in spiritual things, fell gravely ill and the hour of his death arrived. The abbot and all of the brothers gathered around him, to give him courage in his last moments. To their surprise, however, they observed that the brother was facing death with great quietude and calmness of soul.

So the abbot said, "My child, all here know that you were not so diligent in your duties. How is it that you leave for the other life with such courage?"

"It is true, Abba," murmured the dying monk, "that I was not a good monk. I have, however, observed one thing with exactness in my life: I never judged anyone. Because of this, I intend to say to the Master Christ, when I present myself before him, 'You said, Lord, not to judge, in order not to be judged,' and I hope that He will not judge me strictly."

"Go in peace on your eternal journey, my child," the abbot told him with wonderment. "You have succeeded, without toil, in saving yourself."

* * *

Abba Iperechios gives the following counsel to those who are abstinent and practice fasting: "Eat meat and drink wine and do not devour your brother's flesh with slander."

And further: "By slandering God, the serpent was able to cast the first-created out of Paradise. He who slanders his neighbor does the same thing; he burdens his own soul and leads the one who listens to him to evil."

* * *

A holy elder, seeing with his own eyes a certain brother fall into deep sin, not only did not judge him, but wept and said: "He fell today; without doubt I will fall tomorrow. But he certainly will repent, whereas for myself, I am not so sure of this."

* * *

"If you are ever slandered," Saint Ephraim the Syrian writes, "and your innocence is (subsequently) revealed, do not be arrogant. Serve your Lord with humility and thank him for freeing you from the calumnies of men, observing his commandments faithfully and from the heart."

* * *

"If a Christian," Abba Agathon said, "kept the judgment which follows death in mind every moment, he would not sin with such ease."

* * *

A hermit, who was living the ascetic life in the desert of Jordan, had not been tempted by the devil for many years. This had given him courage, and he frequently asserted that the enemy would not dare to tempt strugglers, but went only to those who were negligent and lazy. Once the devil appeared before him and complained to him: "What have I done to you that you play me down so? Did I ever tempt you?"

"Get out of here, evil spirit," the hermit fearlessly yelled, picking up his staff to strike him. "You have no right to bother the servants of Christ. Go to those who invite you with their inattentiveness."

"So that is what you think?" the devil said maliciously. "Do you think I will not find an opportunity, in the forty years you still have to live, to prove you wrong?"

Sure, now, that the bait had all but succeeded, the devil became invisible, leaving a shuddering laugh in the air. From that moment, then, the hermit's thoughts were confused.

"Forty more years of life; o, that is an awfully long time!" he said to himself continually. Then, after a while: "Should I not go into the world to see my relatives? Let me give my tormented body a little rest. When I return, I will continue my ascetic life. I have years before me..., forty years of life!"

He came to a decision and one morning, with his staff in his hand, he set out for the city. But God, in his benevolence, regretted the loss of so many years of labor and sent his angel to stop him.

"Where are you going, Abba?" the angel asked, stopping him on the road.

"To the city," the hermit hastened to say.

"Dear man, now, at the end of your life, you let the devil deceive you? Hurry and return to your hut and bemoan your foolishness, before it is too late for you."

Embarrassed by his setback, the old hermit returned to his cell and died three days later.

* * *

The man who succeeds in having death continually before his eyes conquers faint-heartedness," an elder said to the younger brothers, who asked him for some beneficial advice. And another time, as he was spinning, he assured them: "I have brought death to mind as many times as this spindle has turned, up to the present."

* * *

"When you undertake to begin any task whatever," a certain elder advises, "conscientiously ask yourself this question: 'If I were visited by the Lord at his moment, what would I do?' Take care to listen well to what your conscience answers you. If it reproves you, immediately forsake what you had decided to do and begin some other task of which it approves and which, so as assuredly to complete it, is intrinsically rewarding. The virtuous worker must at every moment be ready to face death.

"When you fall into your bed to sleep, or get up from sleep, when you eat or work, when you are thinking or your mind is idle, constantly say to yourself: 'If the Lord were to call me at this moment, would I be ready?' Listen also with care to what your conscience tells you and do not fail to comply with its directions. Your heart will, indeed, assure you that God has had mercy on you."

* * *

"Take away temptations and no one will be saved" (Abba Evagrios).

* * *

In modern times, a rich man told a certain monk of his philanthropy: "I have given away most of my riches, so that, without growing a beard, wearing monastic garb, and sacrificing myself, I have done everything that is needed to be saved. In essence, I have gained monasticism without your abnormal way of life."

Remembering the words of Saint Basil regarding a great official who had abandoned his wealth, yet kept some money for his needs and had no desire to submit himself to monastic discipline, the monk answered the rich man as Saint Basil did the ancient official: "You have given up your senatorial rank, but you have not become a monk."

* * *

A present day monk tells the following beneficial story: "I was once walking with a very pious and humble man, when we were stopped on the street by an old man distributing small pamphlets. The old man asked us, 'Are you saved? Have you accepted Jesus?'

"My humble companion said, 'I only know that I am a sinner.'

"The old man answered my friend: 'Jesus has saved me. I have the assurance of his salvation. I have conquered pride, lust, and sin. Praise God.'

"At these words, my companion very abruptly grabbed me by the arm, saying to the old man, 'Leave us alone.' But as we walked my humble friend began to cry bitterly. Embarrassed that others were watching, he controlled himself.

"I asked him: 'Why are you crying like this?'

"He quietly answered, 'As that man told us that, a strange voice in my mind translated his words, so that he said, "I have saved myself. I have assured myself. Pride, lust, and sin no longer bother me, for they have conquered me. God must praise me." The mere thought of his blasphemy and the state of his soul crushed me. God forgive us all.' "

* * *

When Arsenios the Great fell ill and understood that at last he had reached the end of his earthly life, he began to cry.

"Are you afraid, Abba?" his disciple asked with perplexity.

"This fear, my child, has never left my heart, since the time I became a monk," this great friend of God answered, his wise lips closing forever.

* * *

"A Christian has great difficulty in attaining three things," Abba Isaias the Anchorite says, "grief (over sins), tears, and the continual memory of death. Yet these contain all of the other virtues."

Of the remembrance of death specifically, he writes: "He who succeeds in saying each day to himself, 'today is the last day of my life,' will never willingly sin before God. He, however, who expects to have many years to live, without fail entangles himself in the nets of sin. God sanctifies the soul which is always prepared to give an accounting for its deeds. Whoever forgets the Judgment remains in the bondage of sin."

* * *

A monk in our times tells us that his own grandfather, who had wished to be a monk, but turned against his deep desire, told him the follwing before he died: "All that has befallen me is the result of a wrong choice. God placed it in my heart to be a monk, yet I ignored Him. I introduced my family to other faiths. Out of my many children, few lived. My wealth brought me no happiness. And now my mind and body are wasted. By removing myself from His grace, I lost the knowledge of God. I willingly cast myself into the cruelty of a demonic world. I only hope that, not blaming Him for my suffering, God will have compassion on me and call me in my heart, at my last breath, once again."

* * *

An old hermit once became gravely ill. He had no one to take care of him. With great difficulty, he would fix a little food for himself, thanking God for the trial which He had sent him. An entire month passed and no one knocked at his door or brought him relief. God, however, saw his patience and sent a divine angel to serve him. In the meantime, the brothers remembered the old hermit and went to his hut to see how he was. As soon as they knocked on the door, the angel withdrew.

From inside, the hermit shouted pleadingly: "For the love of

God, go away from here, brothers.''

They, however, hastily opened the door to see what had happened, and he shouted: ''For thirty days I suffered completely alone and no one thought to come to see me. So, the Lord sent me an angel to keep me company. And now you come and chase the angel away.''

And as soon as he said these things, the elder died in a sweet manner.

* * *

One Father says: ''The nearer a man draws to God, the more he sees himself a sinner.''

* * *

''Happy is the monk who considers himself the outcast of all,'' says another Father.

* * *

One holy woman tells us: ''Imitate the publican and you will not be condemned along with the Pharisee.''

* * *

A modern monk heard it said, and taught his brothers, that money is like manure. Unless it is quickly spread around, it does no good, but scorches and defiles what it covers.

* * *

A monk in our day tells us that he was taught the following by something internal: ''Taking pride in not accepting money from others leads one to far worse sins than greed. Accepting money too willingly from others leads to pride and greed. This is why it is said that evil is rooted in money.''

* * *

One of the Fathers of the desert offered the following vivid lesson to the younger monks: "Imagine, my brother, that at this moment I am taking on the person of the just Judge, and I am ascending the throne of judgment. Then I ask you, 'What do you want me to do with you?' If you were to say, 'have mercy on me,' I would reply, 'and you have mercy on your brother.' And if, further, you told me, 'forgive me,' I would answer, 'and you forgive the faults of your neighbor.'

"Is the Judge perhaps unjust? God forbid!

"Brother, gaining the sympathy of the Judge is in your hand: it is enough to have learned to forgive."

* * *

"A monk," said one of the ancient Fathers, "means a truthful mouth, a holy body, and a pure heart."

* * *

A brother went to consult a certain elder: "Is it all right, Abba, for me to keep two gold coins which are left over from my handicraft sales, so as to have them for my old age, or if I happen to get ill?"

"No, it is not at all correct for you to keep them," the elder answered, "for in this way you learn to set your hopes on them and cease to have the protection of God."

* * *

A monk who fled from the unholy attacks against Orthodoxy in present-day Eastern Europe said the following: "There they threatened us and almost took our lives. We lost our mothers, our fathers, our sisters, and our brothers. We lost our homes and our worldly hopes. But here, many times, we are now losing more than that. We are not allowed to be what we are. Calling what we were monstrous, because they have no spiritual eyes, they call what we are now nothing. May God save us from then and from now.''

* * *

A certain simple believer in our own times told the following:
"I once went to a beautiful church with some friends. The music was melodious. The priest was pious and learned. The faithful were orderly, very pious in their behavior, and quiet. My friends were very moved and spoke continuously of their experience that day.

"Yet another time, I was in a small, humble church. The priest of the church was negligent in his spirituality. The psalmody was not pleasing. The faithful constantly talked and moved about. They seemed uninterested, if not distracted. The friends I had with me were disgusted by these circumstances.

"At the first service I felt a warmth and happiness in seeing my friends happy with the church. I felt proud. At the second service, I felt shame. I was embarrassed by the behavior of the faithful and I was deeply shaken by the disappointment of my friends.

"Asking that God forgive me for this revelation, there were other differences between these two services. At the first, beautiful service, I had tears in my eyes, as did many others. I looked up and imagined that I could see angels above me. At the second service, my eyes were almost completely dry. I thought of nothing above me. Yet, at the second service, my heart was burning with tears and I felt the souls of those who worshipped with me. Truly on every side, in our midst, were beings so gentle and full of peace that I was lost in wonderment at God's beauty. I did not see the external irregularities.

"Such is the strange chasm which separates the beauty of men from the beauty of God.''

* * *

SECTION 7

A certain elder, who was asked by the brothers what condemnation is and what it means to speak ill of another, gave the following explanation:

"In the case of speaking ill of someone, one reveals the hidden faults of his brother. In the case of condemnation, one censures something obvious. On the one hand, if someone were to say, for example, that such-and-such a brother is well-intentioned and kind, but lacks discretion, this would be to speak ill of him. If, however one were to say that so-and-so is greedy and miserly, this is condemnation, for in this way he censures his neighbor's deeds. Condemnation is worse than speaking ill of another."

* * *

A young monk went to consult a certain spiritual elder.

"I fulfill all of my monastic duties," he told him, "and then some; nevertheless, my soul finds no peace. I receive no consolation from God."

"You live according to your own will—for this reason all of these things occur to you," the elder explained to him.

"What must I do, then, Abba, to be at peace?"

"Go find an elder having the fear of God in his soul. Surrender yourself to him in all that he wishes and let him guide you, as he sees fit, to the path of God. Then your soul will find consolation."

The youth listened to the elder's advice and his soul found

peace.

* * *

A modern elder said: "Any man who thinks that he can solve his own problems is like a bird which intends to fly without wings."

* * *

An inexperienced monk consulted a certain insightful elder regarding what rule of fasting he should follow.

"Avoid excesses, my child," he advised him. "Many have tried to fast beyond their powers and did not endure for very long."

* * *

A young monk, going down from the skete to the city, passed by the hut of Abba Ammoun and confessed to him: "My elder, Abba, is sending me to the city on an errand. I, however, who am a man of weakness, fear temptation."

"Be obedient," the holy man advised him, "and if temptation should arise before you, say these words: 'O God of powers, through the intercession of my spiritual Father, deliver me.' "

The brother took courage from the words of the Abba and went immediately about his duty. The devil, however, who had been biding his time to bring harm to the monk, sent a woman of evil ways hastily to entrap him in her evil den. In his despair, the monk suddenly remembered the advice of Abba Ammoun and shouted with faith: "O God of powers, through the intercession of my spiritual Father, deliver me."

He then found himself, without knowing how, on the road that led to the desert.

* * *

The following is an excerpt from a letter of Saint Basil the Great to a certain noble patrician:

"It is good and profitable to communicate everyday and to partake of the holy Body and Blood of Christ, for He Himself tells us: 'Whoever eats my Body and drinks my Blood has eternal life!' Who, then, doubts that partaking continually of life means nothing other than having manifold life? We, here, have the custom of communicating four times a week; namely, Sunday, Wednesday, Friday, Saturday, or any other day on which the memory of a Saint falls."

* * *

"It is not wise," Abba Isaias the Anchorite writes, "for anyone to know how to converse masterfully. Wisdom is to know when to talk and what to say. Appear to be ignorant, in order to save yourselves many pains. He who thinks himself very learned has many fruitless worries. Do not boast of great learning, for the things which you do not know are more than those which you have learned."

* * *

A holy archbishop in our own times gave the following advice to a young monk regarding the monastic style he should follow:

"Seek humility at all costs. Those who have attained the highest degree of humility are the 'fools for Christ,' who, in order to hide their great spiritual gifts, let others believe that they are fools. But in these days, when arrogance is epidemic, there are many who, if they try this monastic path, will become proud in being fools. It is too easy for Satan to make their hidden motives public. And there is always the temptation for the fool to disclose his monastic style or *podvig* to a few, in order to release himself from this hard path. I would, therefore, advise anyone who wishes to undertake this path to do it in an even deeper way. Do foolish things, but be ever so obvious, so that others perceive that you are pretending foolishness. In this way you will be judged as spiritually naive and deluded. Everyone will curse you. And you will have succeeded in the very thing to which the 'fools' of times past aspired. At every moment you must know that the warfare of the devil against the monk is especially strong today."

* * *

"However much you may toil in scattering seed on the path that you walk on, not a green leaf will grow. As well, as much as you labor to cultivate a heart weighed-down with worldly cares, you toil in vain; it is impossible to foster virtues there. For this reason the Fathers chose to leave the world," a certain Abba says.

* * *

"When the Hebrews ceased being occupied with labors for the Egyptians, and lived in tents, they learned to worship God," said a wise Father. "And ships do business and make profits in the harbor, not on the open seas. It is the same with the soul; if it does not cease being occupied with worldly things and does not stay in a quiet place, it neither finds God nor acquires virtues."

* * *

"True escape from the world is for a person to know how to control his tongue, wherever he might be," Abba Tithoes said.

* * *

A young disciple, seeing his elder frequently withdraw deep into the desert, asked him with perplexity: "Why, Abba, do you avoid people? Is it not of greater value when, staying in the world and facing evil and sin, one abhors them?"

"Listen, my child," the kind elder explained to him: "Until one reaches the stature of Moses, becoming deified, he receives no profit from his relations with the world. I, the unfortunate offspring of Adam, suffer frequently that which my father suffered. The moment I behold the fruit cf my disobedience, I desire it, I taste it, and I suffer. In the desert, one does not easily find material things to feed the passions and they are, therefore, more likely to die.''

* * *

One of the Fathers at a certain skete had the gift of clairvoyance. When a gathering (monastic council) took place and the Fathers discussed spiritual matters, he would see angels around him, applauding them. When the discussion turned to worldly matters, the angels withdrew, saddened.

* * *

It was often said of Abba Or by his fellow ascetics that neither a falsehood nor an oath ever came out of his mouth. He never judged another man, nor was he at any time heard to speak, unless it was absolutely necessary.

To his young disciple he used to say: "Take great care, Paul, never to bring outside talk to this cell."

* * *

"With what difficulty I work to control my tongue," a young monk agitatedly said one day to Abba Nistheros.

"When you talk, do you find peace?"

"Never."

"Then why do you talk? Learn to be silent. When it is a matter of something of profit, it is better to listen to others than to speak," the wise elder advised him.

* * *

"He who has learned to be silent has found peace in all things." Abba Poimen likewise says.

* * *

"If you succeed in having God always before you eyes," another Father says, "whether you are lying down to sleep, or rising from your bed, or doing some kind of work, the devil will not dare to harm you. The grace of God will protect you, to the extent that your mind is united with Him."

* * *

"What wretches we are," laments one elder. "We are-ashamed to commit some evil act before men, but we are not afraid or ashamed to act impiously and to sin before God, who knows all of the hidden things of our hearts."

* * *

A certain holy elder once saw the devil with his own eyes and he boldly asked him: "Why do you battle me with such persistence?"

"Because you resist me continuously with your humility," the devil answered, becoming invisible.

* * *

Just as Saint Makarios was returning to his cell one day, loaded down with palm leaves for his handicraft work, the devil stopped him, ready to assault him; but he could not. Some invincible force prevented him.

"You have tormented me a great deal, Makarios," the devil shouted at him fiercely. "I have battled you so many years and yet I cannot pull you down. But what more have you accomplished than I? Perhaps fasting? I, of course, do not eat. Vigils? I do not even need sleep. You have only one threat that frightens me."

"What is that?" the Saint asked with great interest.

"Humility," he unwillingly acknowledged, disappearing.

* * *

"Why does the devil battle monks so passionately?" the brothers asked a spiritual elder. "How does he have such effrontery?"

"If the monks knew immediately how to raise defensive weapons—humility, poverty, and patience—, the devil would never dare to approach them," the elder replied.

* * *

In the last moments of his life, Abba Pambo said these words to the brothers, who surrounded him: "From the time that I became a monk, not even once did I not repent for the words that came out of my mouth. Nevertheless, now that I am going to my Lord, I realize that I have not even made a beginning."

* * *

"Why, Abba, do today's monks, though they toil, not receive the same gifts from God that the ancient Fathers received?" a certain brother asked an elder.

"In ancient times," the venerable elder replied, "there was love between the monks, and each one showed readiness to aid his brother in ascending to higher things. Now love has grown cold and one monk leads another to lower things, and for this reason God no longer grants spiritual gifts."

* * *

Abba John, who was the Abbot of a large monastery in Egypt, once went deep into the desert to meet Saint Paisios, the renowned ascetic, who had struggled alone there for a full forty years.

"What have you accomplished, living so far from people, Father?" Abba John asked him.

"From the time I came here, the sun has never seen me eat," replied the Saint.

"As for me, it has never seen me angry," the Abba said.

* * *

The Patriarch Theophilos of Alexandria once set out to go visit the ascetics at Nitria. On the road, he met an elderly ascetic.

"What have you gained, Abba, living in this solitude?" the Patriarch asked.

"I have come to know myself well," the elder answered, "and I have learned to reproach myself."

"It is impossible for a man to attain any greater profit than this in his life," the Patriarch acknowledged.

When he reached the skete, the Fathers came out to greet him, and each found some word to say to him. Only the holy Pambo stood out of the way, silent.

"Are you not going to say anything to the Patriarch for his benefit?" the elders asked.

"If he does not benefit from my silence, brothers, neither will he benefit from my words," answered the wise Father.

* * *

"Many people," a modern spiritual writer says, "have the virtue of humility in some circumstances. They then succumb to a supposed demand of their social stature or profession and, under the guise of 'social necessity' or 'professionalism,' become arrogant in other circumstances. This is much like mixing soil and water in a container. When the container is untouched and at rest, the soil will settle and the water will remain sweet. But if the container is agitated, then the water and the soil are mixed and become mud. The mud then dries, the water evaporates, and only soil is left. Thus only a person of true peace, incapable of agitation, can actually maintain humble virtue, meanwhile tolerating in himself any ostensibly worldly behavior."

* * *

Yet another spiritual man of our time has said: "When we look down upon any man, because of his color, nationality, or some other shallow thing, we destroy our own souls. Since we are one with all men in Christ, we condemn ourselves when we condemn others. And since the Holy Spirit dwells in all people, when we denigrate anyone for what he is, we blaspheme the Holy Spirit, which indwells him. It is wise for a man, therefore, to avoid anyone who speaks against others because of the color of their skin or because of any other external attribute which God has given them.''

* * *

"My dog,'' Abba Isidoros once said, "is in a more advantageous position than I; for, he has love and he does not have to give a defense for his deeds.''

* * *

"I, too, will go to the place to which the devil will be condemned,'' Abba Poimen said, humbling himself.

Another time he said: "Man needs humility and the fear of God as much as he needs the air which he breathes.''

On another occasion, he said: "The most useful tools for the soul are humility, self-reprobation, and disdain for one's own will.''

* * *

The devil appeared to a very humble monk as an angel of light and told him, in order to pull him down into arrogance: "I am Gabriel and I came to salute you, for you have many virtues and are worthy.''

"Look, you must have made a mistake,'' the humble monk answered, without losing his composure. "I am still living in sin, and for this reason I am not worthy to see angels.''

* * *

In modern times, a novice told his elder: "I am especially prepared for spiritual life, since my family has a history of mystical gifts."

The elder said, "Apparently the only thing that your family has inherited is the condemning pride of Adam. This is the legacy they have left you."

* * *

A certain Christian man went to consult Abba Silouan.

"I have a deadly enemy, Father," he confessed. "The evils which he has brought upon me are innumerable. A short time ago he gained a large piece of my land by deceit. He slanders me wherever he is and he speaks ill of both me and my family. He has made my life unbearable. Now, finally, he is even plotting to take my life. A few days ago, I learned that he attempted to poison me. But he is not getting away with anything else. I have decided to hand him over to the law."

"Do as you like," Abba Silouan told him with indifference.

"Do you not think, Father, that when he is punished, and especially severely, as he should be, his soul will be saved?" asked the man, who was now beginning to show concern for the welfare of his enemy's soul.

"Do whatever gives you peace," the Saint continued to say, with the same air.

"I am going straight to the judge, then," the Christian said, getting up to leave.

"Do not hurry off so," the Saint told him calmly. "Let us first pray for God to bring success on your action."

He began the "Our Father."

"And do not forgive us our trespasses, as we do not forgive those who trespass against us," he heard the Saint saying in a loud voice, as if making an error in this verse.

"You made an error, Abba. The Lord's Prayer is not said that way," the Christian hastened to correct him.

"Nevertheless, that *is* the way it is," the elder answered in all of his impassivity. "Inasmuch as you have decided to hand over your brother to the court, Silouan is offering no other prayer."

* * *

A young monk went to Abba Theodoros of Fermi, to tell him his troubles.

"In the world, Abba, I fasted a great deal, I held frequent vigils, I had tears and contrition in my prayers, and I had in my heart a great passion for every act pleasing to God. Here in the desert I have lost all of these things, and I fear that I will not save my soul."

"That which you did in the world, my son," the wise elder said to him, "was nothing more than a work of vanity, for human praise. God did not accept it. There in the world, the devil did not battle you, nor did he impede your eagerness, since it brought you no profit. Now, however, that you are more decisively enlisted in the army of our Christ, the devil, too, has armed himself against you. You must learn that one psalm said with humility here in the desert is more pleasing to the Lord than the thousands that you said there with vanity; moreover, He receives more gratefully the one day of fasting that you do here secretly than the many entire weeks of fasting that you did in front of others in the world."

"I do nothing now," insisted the youth. "I was better there."

"It is arrogance," Abba Theodoros sternly told him, "that you still think you were better in the world. The Pharisee in the parable of Jesus had the same opinion of himself, and he was censured. Say, my child, that you have never accomplished any good. It is in this way that the tax collector was justified. The sinner, with a broken heart and humble thoughts, is more pleasing to God than a proudly virtuous man."

The elder's lesson, replete with practical experience, brought the young monk to his senses.

As he was saying farewell and leaving, he told him, "Thanks to you, Abba, I have saved my soul."

* * *

A certain elder was asked when one attains humility. "When he remembers his sins continuously," he replied.

* * *

"As the ground on which we walk has no fear of falling," a certain elder said, "so is the humble man."

* * *

Abba Agathon was asked how one manifests sincere love towards his neighbor, and that blessed one, who had attained the queen of the virtues to a perfect degree, answered: "Love is for me to find a leper and gladly to give him my body, and, if possible, to take his."

* * *

"The ancient Fathers," a certain elder said, "when their spiritual work became known to others, saw this not as a virtue, but as a sin."

* * *

"If you are troubled by evil spirits," another Father advises, "reveal them in confession, so as to be released from them quickly. Just as a snake is destroyed as soon as it comes out of its burrow, so an evil thought comes to ruin as soon as it is openly expressed.

"A brother was tormented by carnal desire. For many years, he labored alone, but saw no profit to himself. Finally, in order to conquer his passion, he stood in the middle of the church one Sunday after Liturgy and said loudly, so that all the monks could hear: 'Pray for me, brothers, that God may have mercy on me, because for fourteen whole years I have warred against the flesh.'

"Saying these things, he felt immediately freed from the passion. What he could not do with years of toil and asceticism, confession accomplished in one moment."

* * *

One modern bishop is so accomplished in obedience that,

before he celebrates the Divine Liturgy, he venerates the relics of his elder, contained in the cap of his episcopal walking stick, and asks his blessing to serve. His years of obedience to his spiritual father, who was a simple monk with no priestly orders, have never ceased, even with his elder's death.

* * *

Another holy bishop in our day confided to a monk that, when his spiritual children kiss his hand, he imagines himself under their feet.

* * *

A present-day monk, lamenting the spiritual poverty of the modern age, said that the greatest sin of all is that today we receive the words of the desert Fathers as beautiful rhetoric, yet never heed or live them.

* * *

INDEX